CAN PUBLIC WELFARE KEEP PACE?

CAN PUBLIC WELFARE

KEEP PACE?

MALVIN MORTON, EDITOR

Published for the American Public Welfare Association by
Columbia University Press

1969   NEW YORK AND LONDON

FOREWORD

THE THEME OF THE 1968 FORUM OF THE NA-
tional Conference on Social Welfare, "An Action Platform
for Human Welfare," was a challenge to the American
Public Welfare Association. It was felt that the APWA's
knowledge and awareness of what was happening *inside*
public welfare—experimentation, change, outreach, inclusion—needed to be focused and presented at this Forum.
It was recognized that the Conference theme could inspire
mere platitudes, as themes of some past Conferences had
done, but as an Associate Group, the APWA decided that
it should accept responsibility to apply the theme to what
it knows best—public welfare, at all levels of operation.

With the help of the Association's Board of Directors,
two sessions were planned under the title, "Public Welfare:
Recommitted, Restructured, Revitalized." These sessions,
in which four distinguished leaders in the field presented
papers, were scheduled one after the other on Tuesday
afternoon, May 28. More than five hundred people attended
each session, confirming the belief of the Association that
public welfare is not only in the spotlight, but "on the
spot," in any consideration of such a topic as human
welfare.

The APWA, as in past NCSW Forums, cosponsored several group sessions at the San Francisco Forum—those focused on protective services for children, and for the aged, and on using volunteers. In these sessions, too, it was obvious that new, innovative ways of dealing with problems that dehumanize and disenfranchise people are being used, and that there are many hands ready to help. In these sessions, as in all others, there was awareness of the voices being heard for the first time in concert at a Forum—the young, the militant, the older members—all speaking out of their concern and conviction about human welfare and the institutions which have sanction and responsibility to meet human needs.

Following the Conference, after the selection of papers to be published in *The Social Welfare Forum* and in *Social Work Practice* had been made, the APWA saw the need to publish several papers which had not been included in these two volumes. The papers given by two of the four speakers in the sessions sponsored by the APWA had not been included. (The other two speakers had no written papers to submit, but one of them later wrote a paper for the Association.) The criteria for selection of the papers for this proposed publication were that they have public welfare as a frame of reference, that they deal forthrightly with issues, that they offer constructive suggestions and proposals, and that they view public welfare as one of the basic instruments through which human welfare is safeguarded. Some of the dated matter in the eleven papers selected has been revised and updated to enhance their effectiveness.

The Association wishes to thank the authors, the National Conference on Social Welfare, and Columbia University Press for their help in the publication of this volume, which is a significant other part of the story of the 95th Annual Forum.

GUY R. JUSTIS
Director, American Public Welfare Association

INTRODUCTION

IT IS NOT THE INTENT OF THIS BOOK TO
make public welfare the scapegoat for society's failure to
cope with the root causes of its present crisis. The crisis
has many dimensions, and its impact on human lives can
be measured by many different devices. Since this is the
case, all institutions are involved in the crisis and all must
share the blame for the ghettos—the hunger, the alienation,
the debilitation, the hate—that destroy pride of self-realization and faith in democracy.

The crisis is real. It is all across the land. It is where
children die of lead poisoning and rat bites; where they
burn to death in tenement flats; where they go to sleep in
school because they are hungry; where they become tooth-
less before they reach their teens. It is where some young
men are rejected for military service because they are malnourished and illiterate, and where other young men burn
their draft cards and sit in on college campuses. It is
where professional and white-collar jobs are unfilled, and
where the unskilled are jobless. It is where young people
volunteer to go overseas with the Peace Corps, and where
human services in their own country wait to be done. It is
where the aged poor go hungry and the disabled languish.
It is where people are separated by walls of class, color,

status, hierarchy, and rank, and where all means of communication have been severed.

Public welfare cannot be made the scapegoat for these tragic manifestations of crisis. But it can and should be recognized as one of the involved institutions, both as cause and as solution. It can and must turn the looking glass on itself and be confronted with its red tape, its identification with rules, its preoccupation with forms, its bureaucratic rigidity, and measure their impact on the crisis. At the same time, it must turn the looking glass outward to reveal the countless little acts of love it has performed—acts that were healing, therapeutic, protective, and enabling. Then it must ask itself how and why, and determine its course.

Public welfare can be a powerful change-agent in the crisis, bringing people together to solve problems. It can do more than keep pace. It can lead the way. But to do so, public welfare must be the architect of its own restructuring and the priest for its own recommitment. It must demonstrate that it has the capacity to become the advocate of the hungry and the alienated, providing the means for their wholeness in society. Then its defenders and critics alike will be able to use it as a benchmark for all the rest of society's institutions.

In *Common Human Needs* Charlotte Towle said that public welfare agencies "must continuously have the breath of human life breathed into them." This book is a reminder that the breath of human life in all institutions in a democracy is very dear—particularly so in public welfare.

MALVIN MORTON
Editor

CONTENTS

Foreword   GUY R. JUSTIS   v

Introduction   MALVIN MORTON   ix

The Contributors   xiii

Can Public Welfare Go Where the Action Is?
WILLIAM H. ROBINSON   3

The Public Assistance Power Structure
SYDNEY E. BERNARD AND PHILIP BOOTH   15

Public Welfare—Recommitted, Restructured, Revitalized

     I.   The Commitment   JAMES R. DUMPSON   44

     II.   The Problem   NORMAN V. LOURIE   61

The Long Road from Commitment to Accomplishment
BETTY L. PRESLEY AND HELEN E. KEE   79

On Finding the Older Poor   GENEVIEVE BLATT   96

The New Unionism in the Profession
MITCHELL I. GINSBERG AND BERNARD M. SHIFFMAN   104

P. L. 90-248 and Homemaker Services   EUNICE MINTON   118

Integrating the Rural Welfare Department into the Community   HANS S. FALCK   134

Why Public Welfare Needs Volunteers
CYNTHIA R. NATHAN   151

Next Steps for Children   WILBUR J. COHEN   163

THE CONTRIBUTORS

SYDNEY E. BERNARD, Associate Professor of Social Work, School of Social Work, University of Michigan, Ann Arbor

GENEVIEVE BLATT, Assistant Director, Office of Economic Opportunity, Washington, D.C.

PHILIP BOOTH, Lecturer in Social Work, School of Social Work, University of Michigan, Ann Arbor

WILBUR J. COHEN, Professor, School of Social Work, University of Michigan, Ann Arbor

JAMES R. DUMPSON, Dean, School of Social Service, Fordham University, New York

HANS S. FALCK, Professor of Social Work, School of Social Work, University of Maryland, Baltimore

MITCHELL I. GINSBERG, Administrator, Human Resources Administration, New York

HELEN E. KEE, Project Director, Department of Public Social Services, Marin County, San Rafael, Calif.

NORMAN V. LOURIE, Deputy Secretary, Pennsylvania Department of Public Welfare, Harrisburg

EUNICE MINTON, Consultant, Federal-State Project on Case and Administrative Service System, Children's Bureau, Department of Health, Education, and Welfare, Washington, D.C.

CYNTHIA R. NATHAN, Director, Office of Citizen Participation, Social and Rehabilitation Service, Department of Health, Education, and Welfare, Washington, D.C.

BETTY L. PRESLEY, Director, Department of Public Social Services, Marin County, San Rafael, Calif.

WILLIAM H. ROBINSON, Director, Illinois Department of Registration and Education, Chicago

BERNARD M. SHIFFMAN, Deputy Administrator, Human Resources Administration, New York

CAN PUBLIC WELFARE KEEP PACE?

CAN PUBLIC WELFARE
GO WHERE THE ACTION IS?

WILLIAM H. ROBINSON

CAN PUBLIC WELFARE KEEP PACE?
This is a question that must be carefully defined and a question that must be answered in terms of the political and social situation in which we exist today. Too, it must be answered in terms of who the poor are: 35 million people living abjectly below the poverty line—11 million families, 16 million children.

Let me say quite simply that the answer is "Yes"—if we are given the means. Unfortunately, such a facile answer is almost a tautology, for given the time and the means, we can accomplish all of our realistic goals. The problems that arise revolve around disagreements as to what is reality, around the fact that all too often we procrastinate and run out of time, and finally the fact that the available means are only a part of the whole and the pie must be cut some way and somehow. Thus, we must establish a practicable framework for our priorities.

We are all acquainted with the almost infamous Social

Security amendments of 1967. But to understand those amendments one should have heard Senator Russell Long refer to Aid to Families with Dependent Children (AFDC) mothers as "brood mares" and heard him state that if these women could stage a sit-in at his office, they could do a full day's work. One would have had to read the report of the hearings and the Congressional comment upon the various testimonies to fully comprehend their import. These comments can be summed up quite simply. They said to us in public welfare: "In 1961 you came to Congress with a program for massively expanding the social services to be made available to clients and to expand massively the work and training programs. You stated that with these tools you really could come to grips with the problems of welfare. Well, in 1962 we gave you your public welfare amendments and you hailed them. But what has happened since then? The number of those who receive assistance has done nothing but rise. Now, we are going to do it our way."

Let me state immediately that I do not believe that the public welfare amendments of 1962 (or, for that matter, the Economic Opportunity Act, which we also supported and which is receiving similar treatment in Congress) have been failures. Indeed, I firmly believe that the March of the Poor which took place in 1968 can be directly related to the development of programs under these two pieces of legislation. I believe that the March of the Poor was good, for it developed pressures that can be used in obtaining the one essential that Congress and many state legislatures have not given us: adequate funds to carry out the programs we proposed and adequate funds to guarantee a national standard of assistance. I believe that the increase in the number who receive assistance is related to factors other than a failure of services, a failure of family planning, a failure of training. I believe that it can be directly related to a rising social consciousness in our society, to a growing realization that it is a duty for society to give assistance to all those in need and that the money should not be disdainfully given from a sense of *noblesse oblige,* that the poor as well as the wealthy have rights, and that the poor as well as the wealthy should be able to have some control over their environment and over the design and purpose of their lives.

We are aware of all this, but we must face the political fact that Congress has a quite different view.

Let me be blunt. The freeze on welfare payments written into the Social Security amendments of 1967 represents a conservative conviction by many in Congress (and quite a few outside Congress) that there is a surging tide of immorality among the poor. Although this freeze was slightly thawed by a delay in its effective date, it *was* enacted into law—and should be melted rather than thawed. Whatever the effective date, these legislators believe that illegitimacy and promiscuity among the poor are rife and that they are sins to be stamped out, not social problems to be solved. They wish to embark upon a crusade of "good against evil, light against darkness." They refuse to recognize that today what is needed is a war against the causes of the problems festering in our slums and ghettos and not a war against the helpless individuals who live in them. To these crusaders, the increasing numbers of those who benefit from AFDC result from illegitimacy and an unwillingness or inability to work. To them, a mother's place may be in the home except when she is a poor mother. To them, the whole problem stems from a fatal flaw in the individual and is in no way the result of flaws in the basic fabric of our social and economic structure. Simplifying even more, to them the problem of illegitimacy among the poor means illegitimacy among the blacks, the Spanish speaking, and the Appalachian whites living in our ghettos. Thus the whole problem becomes enveloped by, and complicated by, a conscious or unconscious racism.

It is in these terms that we and the poor will have to march together. We must confront these negative attitudes, recognizing that there are many who have become knowledgeable about the truths of poverty today and who will support us if we propose and develop feasible programs.

What are these programs? First and foremost is education, education for adults and for the young. For the very young, this means an expansion of Head Start to overcome the educational handicaps that limit the chances of poor children. For youth, it means programs to keep them in school and, where these fail, the development of educational and training programs that will prepare them for a role in society. For many of the adults it means combating illiteracy, which is rife in this country.

In the final analysis, we are frequently dealing with the truly hard core of the hard core who must be trained to be trained. If we are to succeed, we must deal with them on an individual, case-by-case basis. The debilitating effects of poverty and the self-image of failure make it difficult for these adults to comprehend all that is involved in steady employment and a regular pay check.

We must be continually creative, recognizing that we are faced with an ever changing group of people in a dynamic economy. This means that we must continually vary and adjust our programs. We must be sure that training is followed by successful job placement. For what response can we expect from clients who have had no involvement, no sense of fulfillment and achievement? This lack of involvement with no sense of fulfillment and achievement must change if people are to be motivated and to feel personal worth and dignity.

We also must stop being defensive when we speak of the high goals toward which we strive. We in the welfare field are often accused of mollycoddling clients. All too often we retreat in the face of these politically motivated accusations instead of saying that we are being realistic in our efforts to help people find meaningful jobs. What we are doing, or should be doing, is to develop education and training programs that take into consideration the abilities of our clients and their educational, economic, social, and psychological backgrounds and disadvantages. We should be proud of doing this.

We should point out to society that the fear of mollycoddling is part of the heritage of this land of opportunity where pioneers once trekked to the West in hope of making their fortunes. But we should also remind those who accuse us of mollycoddling that the Old West is no more. At the turn of the century, the West became settled. During the latter part of this century, those who might have heeded the slogan, "Go West, young man," unfortunately began to abandon the farms and villages, flocking to the cities, and bringing with them their inadequate education and lack of training.

Let us tell it as it is and contrast the "lift-yourself-up-by-your-own-bootstraps" immigrant at the turn of the century with the poor of today. The immigrant to this land of opportunity had certain characteristics. He was probably from Europe, was white, and arrived either alone or with his wife. If he was married and had children, he frequently left his family behind until he could get a toehold. In short, he could take a low-paying job. He could accumulate slowly the passage money for others as needed and, most significantly and most importantly, during that period he could work himself upward so that when the family arrived he would have a decent salary with which to support them. I am not saying that it was all a bed of roses. On the whole, though, the low-paying job was considered a temporary necessity and not a permanent position. The immigrant kept his self-view intact, he retained his self-respect, he had hope, and on all of these things he could build.

On the other hand, what is the background of the people whom we compare with the immigrant? The typical mother in the AFDC program has three or four young children; the typical father in the AFDC of Unemployed Parents program has a wife and four or five young children. So then, we are supposed to put this mother or this father into a dead-end job at $1.35 or $1.60 an hour. They cannot support a family on that.

Let us go further and consider yet another simple fact. What results can we expect from the many hours and days we spend with a man—or a woman—to convince him that he should try again in the educational system that once failed him; from the many hours and days spent with a man—or a woman—to convince him that he can undergo training; from the many hours and days spent with a person already beaten down by past rejections when, at the end of the line, we offer only a dead-end job with an income inadequate to support his family with dignity and with pride?

Let us describe the effects of poverty in still greater detail.

Whatever reservations we may have about the Moynihan Report,[1] there *has* been a breakdown, whatever the causes, in family life among many of the poor. In the case of the deserted mother, there is that simple, deeply felt, and defeating desertion to begin with, compounded by worry about her children and concern over their care. Shall we motivate her to aspire to a dead-end job? What we should be aiming at is bringing these families back together—and they can be brought back together. But we will not accomplish this by offering the father the same hopeless future that may have originally driven him from home. We are not asking a single man, a recent immigrant, with minimal needs to accept a low-paying job. We are asking a man, with a man's dignity, to accept a dead-end, low-paying job and then to say to his family, "I cannot support you adequately." Can we possibly expect success? We are asking this man to raise himself by his bootstraps when he does not even have boots. Or, in the case of the black poor, we are trying to liberate a person who for years has been hobbled by chains, bring him up to the starting line of a race, and then say, "You are free to compete with all the others." Can we honestly believe that this is completely fair? We are asking the poor to build upon hope when they are without hope. We are attempting to build a house on sand.

Let us say to society that all of us must realize the fact that a black revolution is going on in this country. At the same time, we must develop a proper stance on white racism and black power as dimensions of the urban crisis. We must dis-

[1] *The Negro Family: the Case for National Action* (Washington, D.C.: Office of Policy Planning and Research, U.S. Department of Labor, 1967).

cern the nature of the black revolution and assess it for what it is. After hundreds of years of slavery, after years of discrimination, blacks will no longer accept exclusively the low-paying jobs. They are actively searching for the dignity of man, and we will get nowhere if we educate and train without taking that into consideration.

In all of this, we are really talking about the matter of menial jobs and status jobs. Let me define by a simple example what these terms mean to me. Many years ago we employed men in low-paying jobs as "garbage collectors." Today we employ men in high-paying jobs as "sanitation workers." There is the difference.

Quite simply, a menial job is one that does not pay enough for a man or woman to support his or her family in dignity. That is why we are proud that we are attempting to train for status jobs. How does one define a status job? It is a job that pays enough for a man to meet his responsibilities as a man, as a husband, and as a father, and for a woman to meet her responsibilities as a woman and as a mother.

Let us proudly state that we are attempting to match the education, training, and placement programs to the abilities and the total needs of the clients. Let us say to society that to refuse to acknowledge the existence of great and hidden abilities, to refuse to admit the psychological needs of the poor, is to hide from the facts and to guarantee failure. "Let them rake leaves" may have been the answer in the depression; it is not the answer today. Let us declare that we shall structure our programs so that help can be received with dignity—the dignity for which the poor marched.

These must be our goals if we are to keep pace with the poor:

1. Jobs for all who are able to work

Where necessary, the government must become the employer of last resort.

2. Adequate unemployment compensation benefits with built-in education and training programs

3. A guaranteed adequate wage

It is time for society to realize that the validity of an economic adventure need not necessarily be determined by how much profit it will produce, but rather by how many adequately paying jobs it will produce.

4. Family grants

This program would not be adopted to foster dependency but to recognize a universal need for, and the right to, help during the early years of raising a family.

5. Family planning

The right to receive information and guidance in determining the number and spacing of children must be guaranteed to poor families as it is to the more affluent.

6. A comprehensive program to protect and care for all children, particularly those 16 million poor children who are malnourished, ragged, and suffering from undiagnosed diseases and crippling conditions.

When we achieve these goals, then and then only shall we be helping the poor in dignity and in hope. Then we will have a humane welfare system.

But this will take time. There are many other actions that we can and must support.

First of all, we must establish a national standard or level of living beneath which no person in our society will fall. We must insist upon federal guidelines and requirements so that all states will fulfill the minimum standards of health and well-being. One immediate action should be to raise all social insurance benefits under Old-Age, Survivors, Disability, and Health Insurance to this minimum level and, similarly, to transfer all clients of Old Age Assistance, Blind Assistance, and Disability Assistance to the Social Security program so that the basic needs of this large group will be met with dignity. This would make it possible for social workers to concentrate upon the younger fathers, mothers, and their children.

We also must insist that the Department of Health, Education, and Welfare enforce the provisions of the Social Security Act in all states and assure that all eligible persons receive public assistance on a uniform state-wide basis, under a single state-wide agency, without restrictive residence requirements.

We must immediately restore to the assistance rolls all children who have been excluded from the AFDC category because of the "man-in-the-house rule," which was declared unconstitutional in June of 1968.

Let us insist upon an end to the seeming insanity in so many states that places a premium upon broken families instead of united families and make the AFDC Unemployed Parents program a national mandate for every state [2] so that a father need not leave his family to insure their welfare. This program should be expanded to include the underemployed father so that his inadequate income can be supplemented and thus guarantee his children the basic necessities of life.

We must develop paraprofessional jobs in government, industry, and the professions to move indigent persons into

[2] In 1968, only twenty-six states had passed enabling legislation that would allow them to participate in this program.

employment. Each person must be given the opportunity to contribute to society. There exists today a great dearth of professionally trained people. In public welfare we cannot even foresee a time when there will be a sufficient number of trained social workers. Moreover, trained social workers are tied to their desks three and four days a week, trying to get through the paper work, and then they may have to go out into the field in order to get a client to sign a certain document. We need to reassess the priorities for the use of the caseworker's skills and assign specific tasks to subprofessionals. These people are desperately needed. They can be drawn from among the poor. Nurses, too, are desperately needed, and there are few schools in this country that could not use more teacher aides. We not only need to train more paraprofessionals, we need to develop means of using their time and skills more efficiently and establish career ladders for them as incentives to higher achievements.

There is also the desperate need for housing. Should we not demand a decent house for every American family? The supply of housing for the poor must be increased both in and out of the ghetto. The condition of permanently being the renter must be changed. Above all, we must press for open occupancy and home ownership for the poor.

To do these urgent things there must be a new commitment on our part. If we are to march with the poor, keeping pace with them as they go their determined way of deliverance from entrapment in the urban and rural ghettos of this country, we must recapture the heritage of protest and militant action that brought our profession into being.

We must break with the rigid, unyielding system that for so long has kept the poor out of sight and out of mind. The poor march, and we must become relevant to them in their struggle to achieve human decency and dignity. We have to be involved, not merely as sideline watchers of the march. We must offer technical assistance, helping the poor to participate in decisions that affect their lives and their future, to become skilled and sophisticated in the use of power.

If we do not choose to go where the action is, to join with the poor in developing a coalition of mass power to move the social and political structures pitted against change, then we will be sideline watchers—and the poor will march. For they are restless, impatient, and desperately determined.

THE PUBLIC ASSISTANCE
POWER STRUCTURE [1]

SYDNEY E. BERNARD AND PHILIP BOOTH

AMERICAN SOCIETY IS DEBATING its ulti-
mate shape, purpose, and structure. An important part of
that debate deals with issues of public assistance policy.
Shall we be a shared society with a wide variety of life styles
and values built upon a freely available common base of
material well-being? Or shall we freeze into a stratified society with easily identifiable outcasts and deviants—deviants
who are punished through economic deprivation and for
whom even a minimum subsistence is purchased at the price
of social, sexual, and occupational conformity? The crux of
this debate hinges on the extent to which conformity can be
demanded. If everyone can and should support himself, if
those who receive societal benefits ought to repay their ben-
efactors through community service (scrubbing the floors of
the County Building, perhaps, or of the County Commis-

1 The authors are indebted to Gilbert Y. Steiner for his discussion of
the concepts and ideas presented in *Social Insecurity, the Politics of
Welfare* (Chicago: Rand McNally & Company, 1966).

sioner's home), then public assistance's role is to insure this conformity. Social control becomes its primary function.

In a shared society, on the other hand, means will be found via public channels to provide an adequate, universal, minimum income. Among these means, financial assistance dispersed through public welfare agencies would occupy a minor but important place, providing for temporary or unusual circumstances. A shared society would provide nonfinancial services as well, and here public welfare agencies would play a more central role. Public welfare agencies would have social integration as their primary function. For the past thirty years, policy development in public assistance has been characterized by an impasse between the proponents of social control and of social integration.

Professionals, primarily social workers, have attempted to resolve this impasse and to cool its attendant conflicts by rehabilitative services. In a rehabilitative regime, recipients are moved toward conformity (work and self-support) through the use of benign, professionally sanctioned services. With this compromise, financial dependency is not made acceptable as a satisfactory part of social life, nor is conformity imposed by deprivation and scorn.

Explicit examples of these contradictory policies may be seen in comparing the Medicaid program established at the apex year of the contemporary liberal coalition, 1965, with the Social Security amendments of 1967, adopted during a period of abrupt power reversal. Medicaid offered the possibility to include a substantial sector of the population within a broad program covering a central and universal need, medical care. Its potentials for good or ill were quickly revealed by New York's experience.

Moving quickly, New York adopted a program estimated to protect from six to seven million people—perhaps 40 percent of the state's residents.[2] In the political terms herein proposed, New York's Medicaid program would represent an attempt to create a large, powerful constituency, a new economic interest group for public assistance. Two and one-half years later, Governor Nelson A. Rockefeller conceded the failure of this attempt. In early March of 1968, the Governor approved legislation to reduce Medicaid expenditures by an estimated $300 million per year, dropping some 600,000 persons from eligibility for assistance. A year later, the State legislature approved a further reduction in Medicaid, lowering the income eligibility level, and requiring all Medicaid patients except those on welfare and in-hospital patients to "pay 20 percent of their medical costs before they can receive government aid." [3]

The scope of these mid-1960 policy swings indicates, perhaps, the increasing tensions and fissures in American political coalitions.

SOCIAL VALUES AND PROGRAM FUNCTION:
THE BOUNDARIES OF POLICY CHANGE

Public assistance is not the only social welfare program which has been squeezed by America's ambivalence toward

[2] Barbara Callahan, "Legislation Wrap-up," *Hospital Progress,* December, 1966, p. 88; Maurice Carroll, "Stratton Moves to Curb Medicaid," New York *Times,* January 16, 1968, p. 22.
[3] James F. Clarity, "$300 Million Cut in Medicaid Voted . . . ," New York *Times,* February 21, 1968, p. 1; Sydney H. Shanberg, "Welfare Slashed by Republicans in Assembly Vote," New York *Times,* March 30, 1969, p. 1.

its unfortunates. Mental hospitals, prisons, reform schools, all have been caught between the conflicting goals of treatment *vs.* custody, punishment *vs.* reform, or eligibility based solely on need *vs.* such noneconomic criteria as age, residence, sexual continence, and, covertly, race.

While we do not propose to deliver a sermon on values, we shall discuss them here because widely shared values form the basis for support of, or opposition to, specific policies. Measures requiring that Aid to Families with Dependent Children (AFDC) mothers seek employment are supported by widely shared convictions about the character-building function of work as a model of parental behavior,[4] the evils of dependency, and hostility toward the poor and the black.

Such broad social values are translated into political terms through "public opinion." In 1967, most Congressmen, governors, and other observers felt that public opinion demanded some action to check or reverse rising welfare costs. Public assistance had become a central public political issue. The issue had been defined as rising costs, and those who favored restrictive policies tapped latent interest groups who were responsive to values and slogans associated with social control goals. This political situation provided the background and limiting framework within which more highly organized and defined interest groups battled over specific and crucial legislative details. Looking back at the outcome, the ability of the proponents of social control to define the issues and to channel hostility toward the welfare poor allowed them to produce sweeping and repressive policy changes.

4 U.S. Congress, House Committee on Ways and Means, Report No. 544, *Social Security Amendments of 1967*, pp. 3–4.

GOVERNMENTAL STRUCTURE

What is the policy-making structure in which these boundaries of policy change are drawn and redrawn, are held fast or stretched? Who are the major groups and elements within the structure who develop, legitimize, transform, resist, or accommodate policy change?

Major new forces, the urban crisis, the near bankruptcy of state governmental finances, and the militancy of client groups may produce a major revision in the relative influence and likely outcome of current policy conflicts. We think that the policy-makers within public assistance will meet the current crisis in traditional ways. The governmental public assistance structure consists of a federal-state-local system of program administration created by federal and state legislation and financed, in varying proportions, by all three levels of government.

The state level. The key policy decisions which, essentially, determine the aggregate number of assistance recipients and the magnitude of assistance expenditures are set by the state legislative and administrative authorities through definition of eligibility criteria and the level of assistance grants. The legislative appropriation process places limits on state assistance expenditures; in the process, restrictions may be placed upon the size of the state-wide caseload and ceilings on the grants to given classes of households. State government is a major locus of pressures to reduce or accelerate the constant growth in state assistance expenditures. State legislatures operate as a major policy-making center, and state programs tend to reflect their preference for the economical and noncontroversial as well as

their views on program function and legislative priorities,
public assistance *vis-à-vis* health, education, or highways.

The federal level. At the federal level, the Congress
usually gives only a cursory review to the public assistance
program during its annual appropriation process (as dis-
tinct from periodic modification of substantive provisions).
This process is semiautomatic in that the Congress regularly
appropriates the federal matching share of state assistance
expenditures, in accordance with long-standing, open-end
formulas. Although Congress remains free to revise this
formula, long habit, having the weight of tradition, has developed what amounts to a commitment to the states to follow it through without change. Contrary to the pattern in
other program areas and, leaving aside the restrictive
changes incorporated in the 1967 amendments, the Senate
has been the source of innovation and program extension in
public assistance.[5] Senators and Representatives are responsive to their states' requests for more substantial federal
sharing in total costs. This has produced a grant-in-aid formula which redistributes funds from states with high to
those with low per-capita income, but does not provide
strong leverage for states to move from low to higher average monthly grants.[6]

Presidential initiative in extending or revising the program occurs rarely, again unlike the pattern of federal activ-

[5] Steiner, *op. cit.*, pp. 48–63. See discussion, *infra*, of 1967 amendments; also, statement of Senator Fred Harris in support of S.2892,
Congressional Record, January 31, 1968.

[6] The federal share in Old Age Assistance, for example, is 31/37ths
(nearly 84 percent) of the first $37 per month per recipient; for the
balance of the average grant, up to $75, the federal share varies from
50 percent, for states with per-capita income at or about the
national average, to 65 percent, for states with the lowest per-capita
income.

ity in other programs. Presidents Eisenhower, Kennedy, and Johnson have frequently resisted the expansion of public assistance *vis-à-vis* social insurance, with uneven success.

The 1967 amendments were aimed at limiting the growth of federal expenditures in two programs: AFDC, which accounts for one third of the $7 billion total; and medical assistance, the most rapidly growing program, which would have accounted for over $2 billion in 1968 under current legal provisions. Under the new AFDC ceiling, effective July 1, 1968 (but subsequently postponed until July 1, 1969), federal matching is limited to the percentage of children in the state under age eighteen who were receiving assistance because of an absent parent. This action has been appropriately called the first purposively punitive welfare legislation in the history of the United States government.[7] In essence then, we conclude that the long-established pattern of automatic funding and Congressional initiative for incremental increases in the federal matching formula has been drastically broken; it remains to be seen whatever form possible modification of the repressive action of 1967 may take and whether the old pattern will be reestablished.

Notwithstanding the initiative in policy innovation taken by the 1967 federal legislation, it remains exceptional in the program's history. Essentially, policy-making in public assistance is extremely decentralized to the state and local (county) level; such policy shifts as were embodied in the restrictions, ceilings and otherwise, introduced by the 1967 federal amendments leave substantial discretion to state and local agencies in the application of ceilings,[8] and in the de-

[7] Daniel P. Moynihan, "The Crisis in Welfare," *Public Interest,* Winter, 1968, p. 3.

[8] We do not suggest that the degree of state discretion permitted under the 1967 amendments will enable these states to avert the impact

termination, for example, of what groups or classes of AFDC recipients (mothers and children over age sixteen) are appropriately referrable to training or employment.

The degree of discretion exercised by the key official units (county public assistance departments) is also subject to substantial variation, depending, for example, on whether county departments operate under state departmental supervision or under direct state welfare department administration.

The import of decentralization and the variety of state and local policies make state and local institutions obviously attractive targets for change. Change which is brought about in any particular area, however, does not spread evenly or easily throughout the state or national system.

INTEREST-GROUP STRUCTURE

Group theory. We rely heavily on group theory in political science literature as a source of generalization.[9] Policy differences are considered debates over values rather than disagreements over facts, although the role of factual information remains important. Political conflict tends to be carried on through groups and group activity. To achieve influence, that is, to get other people to act, or think, or

---

of federal limitations on matching grants without increasing the level of state assistance expenditures.

[9] See Earl Latham, "The Group Basis of Politics: Notes for a Theory," in Heinz Eulau, *et al.*, eds., *Political Behavior: a Reader in Theory and Research* (Glencoe, Ill.: Free Press, 1956), pp. 232–45; Steiner, *op. cit.*, David B. Truman, *The Governmental Process: Political Interests and Public Opinion* (New York: Alfred A. Knopf, 1962).

feel, as the group intends,[10] the group needs shared identity, attitudes, and values; these, in turn, provide bases for claims on other groups. We think of the "interest" of an interest group as the shared attitude of its members toward whatever constitutes its claims on other groups; when it makes claims upon or through government, it becomes a political interest group.[11] Formal organization constitutes an important stage in interest-group development, and the group's political influence is associated with the degree of organization achieved as well as the effectiveness with which it is used.

In the decision-making process, various key elements play important parts: access to policy-makers; manipulation of formal structures (committee membership and rules); the use of official organizational status or professional role; wealth; delaying or disruptive capacity; leadership; strategy and tactics; goal commitment; and possession of a monopoly of key knowledge and skills. Success in forming alliances with other groups which have similar or compatible claims on government may hold the key to more influence.

In discussing the interest groups, we distinguish between groups for which public assistance is a central or a marginal interest, which manifest an intermittent or continuing interest, and between economic *vs.* noneconomic (ideological) interests in public assistance.

The general public. We suggest that there are no powerful interest groups with a continuing central concern about public assistance policy; and that the program is called to

[10] Edward C. Banfield, *Political Influence* (Glencoe, Ill.: Free Press of Glencoe, 1961), p. 3.
[11] Truman, *op. cit.*, p. 37.

the attention of the general public only intermittently and in crisis situations.[12]

Few people, even among those who may be potential recipients, consider themselves as having strong personal continuing economic or noneconomic interests in the program. A study of unemployed men, first-time public assistance applicants, reports that they saw themselves, typically, as different from the other men in the agency's waiting room; the experience was a blow to their self-concept and identity.[13] Under these quite common conditions, interest groups should have a substantial impact on policy.

ECONOMIC INTEREST GROUPS

Clients should be but are not the major economic interest group in public assistance. They hold few keys to the exercise of political or economic influence. Clients do not possess such important influence-producing assets as organizational skills, wealth, or a monopoly of skill or knowledge.

Within the client group, moreover, the distribution of benefits is closely related to two factors: (1) the possession of "acceptable" reasons for dependency; and (2) membership in a strong organization which encompasses other non-assistance groups.[14] Thus, clients who receive the highest monthly benefits tend to be the blind, whose reasons for dependence fit the above criteria; the lowest monthly benefits go to the AFDC and general assistance recipients.

[12] Other programs, including conservation, water pollution, and recreation, for example, are of little interest to the general public, but they do possess effective "special" publics and stronger client groups.

[13] Scott Briar, "Welfare from Below: Recipients' Views of the Public Welfare System," *California Law Review*, LIV (1966), 370–85.

[14] Steiner, *op. cit.*, pp. 113–15, 153–57.

The recent growth of organized welfare recipient groups suggests that they possess the potentiality of exercising influence on the organization, content, and delivery of welfare services—pointed toward more adequate assistance, delivered in a less degrading manner. The beginning of formal appearances of such groups before Congressional and state legislative bodies forecasts the exercise of influence on legislative policy as well as some adverse reaction by such bodies against "pressure" from a source not previously accepted as possessing legitimate influence.

The major organization of welfare recipients, the National Welfare Rights Organization (NWRO), had made a substantial impact on administrative agencies by the end of 1968. Thus, the new Secretary of HEW, Robert Finch, described the organization as "an important constituency of HEW," following a meeting with its leadership. The secret of the organization's success has been identified as concentration on the specific objective of more adequate levels of assistance and avoidance of "ideas and goals that could become divisive." [15]

Other groups within the public assistance field that have economic interests include professions and agencies supplying health care and social services to public assistance clients. These agencies receive substantial appropriated funds as compensation for their services. Health and medical care, a major component of this aggregation of services, accounted for about $3.5 billion of the $9.9 billion total in fiscal 1967/68. These groups have formed alliances with public assistance agencies based upon shared goals for the expansion of welfare program services. Specialized agencies

[15] John Herbers, "Rights Groups Split . . . ," New York *Times,* March 9, 1969, pp. 1, 69.

concerned with family-planning services and with specific
health hazards, such as blindness and heart disease, have developed substantial constituencies outside the assistance population, while perhaps serving a large number of relief recipients; their latent influence, growing out of recognized
access to important financial resources, and their "potential" for alliance with still other nonideological groups have
made them valuable allies for client groups and public assistance agencies. Their interests, however, lead them to support extensions of services, not increases in the subsistence
grant, and their interest in services may conflict with recipient interest in increased subsistence payments.

GOVERNMENTAL AGENCIES

State and local government public assistance agencies have
organizational interests of both economic and noneconomic
types. County-administered departments, for example, attempt to maximize the state and federal share and to avoid
increasing the local share of total assistance costs. In this
connection, their policies may stress the deterrent function
of the program in order to reduce caseload size and costs.
Other state and local departments, however, maximize federal sharing so as to be able to provide large assistance
grants.

Yet because of their desire for autonomy, all agencies
tend to resist limitations imposed by superior governmental
units on their freedom of action in policy-making and execution; in such instances, they may resist pressures to adopt
more stringent assistance policies, thus illustrating a nonideological defense of organizational independence and autonomy.

The American Public Welfare Association (APWA) is the national organization of administrators, workers, board members, with a scattering of concerned professionals and laymen.[16] The organization attempts to fill two quite different roles, that of influencing national policy as well as that of servicing membership needs. The APWA's ability to influence policy is limited by its relatively small size and the underrepresentation of urban centers. Both these circumstances may be changing. Membership is rising rather rapidly—from 7,700 in 1963 to 10,000 in 1967; possibly this increase reflects changes in composition as well.

The APWA provides an important forum for the various groups interested in public welfare. Its meetings have provided a platform for militant client groups and for the organization of *ad hoc* resistance to, or support of, current controversial issues. Primarily, however, it has served an important function as a mechanism for achieving unity on policy goals among the administrators from the fifty states and for interpreting these positions to appropriate governmental bodies. The innovative impact of the APWA is limited, however, by the diversity in values, career, and policy goals of its membership.

STAFF ASSOCIATIONS

Staff associations (unions), a relatively new development, have so far become units of independent, outside-affiliated

---

[16] This discussion is drawn from *ibid.*, pp. 148–53.

unions only to a minor extent, although those organizations have existed for several decades. Fragmentary data drawn from experiences too brief and localized to warrant generalization indicate considerable variation in goals, from those concentrated on wages, hours, and working conditions, work load, and organizational recognition for bargaining purposes, to those focused on professional status and client-centered concerns. Although staff associations, agencies, and clients have made temporary and fragile informal alliances, recognition by most administrators that staff associations are a source of support in achieving program goals is not likely to take place soon; their contention with one another for power stands in the way.[17]

To sum up, public assistance economic interest groups share relatively few common goals. Client interest in increased grants will often conflict with the immediate goals of the other, usually stronger, interest groups. All interest groups may share the goal of increased services, such as medical care or counseling, but their relative priorities may well differ. In the inevitable compromises of policy-making, clients' goals may be sacrificed more readily than those of other participants.

NONECONOMIC GROUPS

A number of groups share an interest in public assistance policy with administrative agencies and with client groups. Noneconomic ideological interest groups do not see public

17 Bureau of Family Services State Letter No. 985, "Relationships with Representatives of Organized Public Welfare Employees and Recipients," Welfare Administration, U.S. Department of Health, Education, and Welfare, July 31, 1967.

assistance as essential for their survival or for achievement of their primary goals. Involvement in public assistance policy is likely to be based on ideological commitment to such broader goals as community services (League of Women Voters), or reducing government spending (chambers of commerce).

Since public assistance policy is not closely related to their group or organizational goals, these groups display an intermittent and less effective influence on policy-making than otherwise comparable groups with vital, usually economic, interests in public assistance policy. The Nursing Home Association, for instance, is likely to exert a more persistent and informed pressure on Medicaid policy than is the League of Women Voters.

Coalitions and alliances may be enduring or temporary. The most enduring are organized within voluntary planning and coordinating bodies. More temporary coalitions are structured around some immediately pressing issue. Planning bodies such as state welfare leagues are likely to be more persistent and expert in their activities than the *ad hoc* coalitions. Traditional temporary alliances include the National Association of Social Workers (NASW) and staffs and boards of private agencies, who ideally would bring along business and labor support. More recent coalitions depart from this traditional pattern as client groups and students have come to take active roles. In one case, clients and county department staff joined in resistance to a proposal to move the county welfare office from the centrally located county courthouse to a remodeled garage at the edge of town. In this situation, activist university and social work students working with AFDC-NWRO mothers were allied with a loose coalition of clergymen, the local NASW chap-

ter, civic-minded lay groups, and a few social work professionals and members of the School of Social Work faculty.
Here, the economic interests of clients and the professional
status and self-interest of agency staff were allied with the
ideological humanitarian interests of other groups. Conspic-
uously absent from the coalition, however, were voluntary
social agencies, most social workers, business and labor
groups, and the great bulk of the "respectable" social welfare community.

While the impact of these groups may be, and in this case
was, substantial in effecting particular improvements and
even more substantial in blocking backward steps, such as
the imposition of numerical or monetary ceilings, that impact cannot be used to produce major continuing changes
in public assistance policy. The alliance noted above
quickly came undone some months later on the occasion of
a new local crisis, when the NWRO groups and students
publicly criticized agency staff members in a successful effort
to obtain increased clothing grants.

Among opposing groups, some business groups have seen
the rising level of assistance expenditures as thwarting their
desire to check spending and tax increases. Their influence
has been effective, from time to time, when allied with that
of political leaders who appealed to the social control function of public assistance—when they asserted that the policies responsible for higher expenditures were fostering immoral behavior and undermining the incentive of parents,
especially fathers, to support their children and the mothers
of their children. Yet their interest, though continuing, has
not tended to be sustained or profound.

Finally, among groups with ideological interests, the
NASW claims a preeminent role as a public assistance

spokesman. But, as noted, public assistance tends to be an ideological rather than a directly economic issue for the bulk of its membership. Only 5 percent of the public assistance staff are members of NASW, and only 7.4 percent of all NASW members staff public assistance agencies.[18] On both counts, obviously, public assistance is a minor interest of NASW members.

We have noted that interest-group structure is unstable, often varying with issue and program. Public assistance supporters find that change-oriented coalitions are not lasting, and soon disbanded. The groups with major program interests (and often a primary commitment to the *status quo*) resume ascendancy and reorient policy.

POLICY ROLE OF OFFICIALS

Our basic thesis is that the single most influential interest group in the public assistance structure is the executive staff of the state welfare departments. Governors or legislators may well have greater decision-making power over a specific issue or occasion, but in the long run, the central administrative staff's capacity to influence decisions outweighs that of the others. This generalization must be qualified to take account of differential influence over given types of decisions. Thus, the total appropriation for public assistance in any year may reflect decisions made by governors and legislators to a greater extent than those of administrators. The distribution of that largesse in respect to such a basic matter

18 U.S. Department of Health, Education, and Welfare, *Closing the Gap . . . in Social Work Manpower,* Report of the Department Task Force on Social Work Education and Manpower, Office of the Under Secretary (Washington, D.C.: U.S. Government Printing Office, 1965), Table 9, p. 34.

as the maximum grant can be determined by either legislative or administrative decisions. Recent evaluations of the budgetary process indicate that the best single predictor of the size of an appropriation is the previous year's amount. This amount is shaped over time by the pattern of agency requests, so that even here the administrators exert substantial influence upon the outcome.[19]

Decisions which do not involve identifiable appropriations—staffing patterns, training procedures, the "climate of service"—have considerable policy impact and are almost totally within the administrative prerogative.[20] Most crucially, decisions embodied in the initial drafting of legislative proposals and the interpretation of enactments fall within the bureaucratic orbit. A case in point is the advice to state welfare agencies by the Department of Health, Education, and Welfare on the impact of the language of the 1967 Social Security amendments regarding the so-called "AFDC freeze." The states were advised, in effect, that they did not have the option of reducing their active caseload by maintaining waiting lists or "discontinuing assistance for the excess cases." [21]

We have indicated that other interest groups are rela-

[19] Ira Sharkansky, "Four Agencies and an Appropriations Subcommittee: a Comparative Study of Budget Strategies," *Midwest Journal of Political Science*, IX (1965), 254–81; Aaron Wildavsky, *The Politics of the Budgetary Process* (Boston: Little, Brown, 1964).

[20] Charles I. Schottland reminded the NCSW two years ago of the key importance, too often overlooked, of decisions of budget officers and other operating officials. See Schottland, "Administrative Decisions and Fund Allocation in Social Welfare," in Leonard H. Goodman, ed., *Economic Progress and Social Welfare* (New York: Columbia University Press, 1966), pp. 65–91.

[21] Unnumbered State Letter, "Social and Rehabilitation Service, Subject: Limitation on Federal Sharing in AFDC-Public Law (90-248)," signed, Mary E. Switzer, Administrator, S.R.S., January 22, 1968.

tively less powerful because of their lack of political resources, or because of the episodic and peripheral nature of their concern with public assistance policy. As a group, state executives possess considerable political resources. Among them are individuals with extensive commitment to the field, in terms both of careers and of values. The bulk of detailed policy and program expertise is still theirs. Few legislators make public assistance an area of expertise, although those who do so wield substantial influence upon the voting behavior of their colleagues.[22] There are a few academics, reformers, and practicing social workers with a solid grasp of this policy area. Their numbers are small, and they often share goals, priorities, and value assumptions with this highly committed segment of public assistance administrators.[23] In addition to commitment and expertise, the administrators have unparalleled access to governors, legislators, and other key governmental decision-makers. Not only the most legitimate, they are often the only source of detailed information on policies, procedures, problems, and alternatives. Breaking this monopoly of access to or mastery of information can be the means whereby an outside group secures some influence. This may, in part, explain the sharpness of the battle for access to a manual or handbook, and the emphasis on "know your rights" and on legislative detail which fill the NWRO's National Welfare Leaders Newsletter.

22 See Steiner, *op. cit.*, on the role of Senator Robert Byrd, p. 157, and Nicholas, A. Masters, *et al.*, *State Politics and the Public Schools: an Exploratory Analysis* (New York: Alfred A. Knopf, Inc.; 1964), for similar situations in education policy.

23 A recent review of welfare policy by Moynihan (*op. cit.*) asserts that the period of policy dominance by professionals and officials is ended.

So far, we have spoken of state officials as if there were no important differences among them, except that some are more highly committed to the policy area than others. In fact, the fifty state directors come from diverse backgrounds, share no uniform sense of professional identity or values, and support only a minimal set of shared policy goals. As state directors, they agree as to the importance of additional federal funds, of increased state autonomy, and applaud such generalized goals as the extension of social insurance and family-centered social service programs.

As a group, their strongest identification will be with their state and their organization. In terms of career and professional background, we can start with the fact that in 1964, only 5 percent of all public assistance employees had a master's degree in social work; a further 20 percent had some graduate education in a school of social work. Most of these employees were in administrative positions. More specifically, one fifth of the state directors had M.S.W. degrees or the equivalent,[24] and we think it probable that at other state-level staff positions the proportion was even higher. However, it must be clear that the highest proportion in any position was 30 percent and hence probably no more than one fifth to one third of those holding administrative positions were graduates of schools of social work.[25]

Who are the others, the vast majority of officials? At the state director level they include a group of career officials who derive their skill and expertise from experience on the job but may possess little formal social work or other profes-

[24] We do not suggest that directors would follow different policy lines if they possessed the M.S.W. degree, even though they would be likely to have a different professional identification.

[25] *Closing the Gap in Social Work Manpower,* pp. 13–16, 22–24.

sional training. Others are political appointees whose commitments are to the governor, party, and political career,
though not necessarily in that order. Though for different
reasons, these two occupational types, the political ap-
pointee and the experience-trained bureaucrat, are not
likely candidates for policy innovation.[26] The former is
particularly subject to pressure to place immediate political
needs ahead of long-term agency policy goals. The bureaucrat is likely to resist nonincremental and unfamiliar policy
innovations derived from experiments or experiences in
other fields. The impact on long-term policy of the ap-
pointee with a political career is likely to be slight. Turnover in the state director position is about 50 percent every
two years and is probably associated with changes in political control, according to APWA information. Turnover
among state headquarters administrative staff below the director level is likely to be lower, and this cadre of executives
who have often been trained on the job have expertise
which is highly specialized, and not readily transferable
from traditional services and approaches to new ones which
are proposed.[27] The extent to which this description char-
acterizes all, some, or a few current agency staff members is
an appropriate area for further study. The state-level staff
increased by 28 percent between 1962 and 1965, though
turnover rates may have been as high as 20 to 25 percent.[28]

It is likely that the effect of the combination of greater
numbers and high turnover has raised the number and pro-

26 Robert A. Scott, "Selecting Clients for Welfare Agencies," *Social
Problems*, XIV (1967), 253–55.

27 *Ibid.*

28 Division of Research, Bureau of Family Services, U.S. Department
of Health, Education, and Welfare, *Public Welfare Personnel, 1965*
(Washington, D.C.: Welfare Administration, 1967), Tables 2 and 6.

portion of those who have formal social work training. If so, this increased professionalization *may* produce greater group cohesion and consistent effort toward national policy goals. The turnover accentuates the influence of the experienced career group within public assistance. That relatively small group who have achieved long tenure, expertise, and high position will have an impact on state and national policy incommensurate with their numbers. Well known to each other, sharing career commitments and, often, social work professional training, they are called on for individual consultation, to submit testimony before Congressional committees, and to man formal and informal policy advisory bodies by the federal agency, NASW, APWA, and *ad hoc* and continuing ideological interest groups. Nor is their political impact limited to the federal administrative level. It is probably most effective, and often crucially so, in their states' delegation in the Congress. This group represents the model of administrators in policy-making.

PREFERRED STRATEGY AND TACTICS

Incrementalism and small-scale, continuous changes in a previously set direction constitute the typical pattern of program change. Social workers are frequently criticized for their adherence to this model. However, we stress that incremental changes are the rule in most areas of social life, certainly in large-scale governmental programs. But no one would wish to emulate the annual model changes in automobiles and household appliances in seeking large-scale continuous innovations.

Granting the incrementalist bias, can one devise strategies which speed up incremental changes?

Conflict reduction. This is the traditional strategy which we feel has characterized public assistance.

Caught between conflicting goals—"provide service and minimize cost"—program administrators do not publicize their program and its benefits, and especially not to prospective recipients. Success stories, such as that of the mother who finishes college, can be publicized by the social insurance program, but they raise too many questions among non-college-graduate state legislators who question AFDC as a channel for subsidizing scholarships. Conversely, rising caseloads and costs are highly visible. Should he wish to use AFDC to facilitate a recipient's education, the administrator's strategy more likely would be to change a rule and omit public announcements. Better the uneven application of a "good" rule than the uniform application of more restrictive policies.

There is almost complete agreement among observers of public assistance that first priority should go to increasing grants to recipients, and there is similar agreement on the political difficulty of achieving any substantial increase. Grant increases are very expensive. In 1967, Michigan removed AFDC ceilings, adding an average of only $12 to the monthly family grant but increasing annual outlay by $5 million. This is part of the brutal arithmetic which encourages attention to expansion of nonfinancial services. Many incentives lie in this area: a very favorable 3 to one federal matching formula, federal requirements of worker/caseload and worker/supervisor ratios; increases in staff size, pay, or supply of technical skills approved by staff and administrators. Some program supporters outside the agency may feel that services are all or part of the answer to the welfare problem. Administrators who hold this view do not choose

services over assistance, but pragmatically choose the area
which promises the greatest immediate program expansion
and the least resistance.

A third conflict-reducing technique consists of transform-
ing value and goal issues into technical issues. Few policy
areas are as technically forbidding or as pregnant with policy implications as the details of the federal-state matching
formulas. A major program policy change was brought
about when the matching formula was changed to require
matching the state-wide average payment rather than each
individual recipient's payment. The more generous federal
share increased the amount of money available to the states
for grants to recipients.

Conflict risk. Conflict-risking, constituency-creating strategies have also been used. They are characterized by aggressive efforts to interpret the agency's program to a wide
public audience, using speeches, news releases, advisory
committees, and, most recently, client advisory groups.
Wildavsky [29] offers a fairly complete listing of such strategies: seeking out and involving legislators and other key decision-makers through the visitation program in which community leaders accompany caseworkers to a client's home;
providing visible services to clientele and notifying them of
benefits provided; expanding clientele, such as New York's
efforts to include 40 percent of the state population under
Medicaid. It is common for state legislators to be contacted
by disgruntled clients, and few state offices pass a week without replying to the resulting queries. Such queries are given
high priority, and personal visits are often made to the legis-
lator by a staff member. Other techniques include having

[29] Wildavsky, *op. cit.*, pp. 64–127.

satisfied customers write their Congressman; advertising and promoting the most popular subprogram (typically, OAA's popularity carries along other program innovations); using advisory committees, publicizing their reports, and encouraging their members to lobby for the report's recommendations. Some agencies, Wildavsky notes, minimize the appearance of spending by initially asking for less than enough in anticipation of a later supplemental appropriation. Recent experience in Michigan and Illinois suggests that this is a dangerous maneuver.

This listing indicates the tenuousness of an active constituency-creating strategy. Many of the tactics are unavailable to the public assistance executive except in unusual circumstances or are readily applicable only to the most popular and often least visible parts of his program. The most obvious constituency-creating device—expanding clientele and increasing benefits—collides with widely held sentiments that the program is residual and ought in all decency and wisdom to be reduced. Administrators respond by stressing global and unmeasurable benefits, such as job training leading to self-support and strengthened family life, both items in short supply and high demand.

It is our reluctant conclusion that direct efforts by elements of the public assistance political system to build public assistance into an adequate, large-scale, income-maintenance program will not overcome the obstacles we have identified: the absence of a powerful constituency; the fragmented, decentralized structure; and, most importantly, the centuries-old public view that "welfare" is an appropriate agency of social control.

The executives strive valiantly and with some success to overcome these handicaps or to minimize their excesses. Yet we conclude, as have many others, that public assistance can become a useful program only after alternative income-maintenance programs absorb the bulk of its clientele. What strategy might be suggested for this goal?

The power structure is admirably designed to resist basic and fundamental change through the action of any single or likely combination of interest groups. Even the 1967 amendments contain some self-contradictory provisions; they have the primary effect of accentuating and legitimating punitive policies and practices already existing in some states and localities. The states affected most adversely by the reduction in federal AFDC funds are likely to continue to press to reverse the 1967 amendments and will probably have some success. On the other hand, the amendments authorize some progressive "step" changes in other areas, such as doubling child welfare funds and requiring states to offer family-planning service to "all appropriate AFDC recipients."

Revolutions and counterrevolutions are rare, and the one lays the ground for the other. In 1967, conditions for repressive changes were almost ideal with a highly aroused public opinion critical of public assistance and an exceptionally responsive Congress. Yet, the changes were relatively slight; consider, for example, that AFDC was not turned back to the states nor was desertion or illegitimacy made grounds for denial of assistance.

Since direct attacks on disputed policy areas seem unproductive, we suggest a strategy of indirection designed to reduce the visibility of public assistance to hostile interests. A most desirable example would be alternative income-maintenance programs, less vulnerable to political attack. Children's allowances have this quality; the negative income tax probably does not. In either case, the proposed benefit levels do not make either program a likely replacement for public assistance, especially during their initial years. Extension of social insurance by raising minimum retirement benefits to $100 a month, though less glamorous, would have more immediate impact as well as greater political feasibility.

Another long-term suggestion would be a social insurance program to parallel AFDC. This has been called "fatherless child insurance." [30] Divorce occurs at all social levels, and a program to cushion its effects would find supporters among the increasing number of men who cannot support two families at middle-class levels on one middle-class income.

Federal assistance payment standards, accompanied by federal payment of a national minimum grant level, as recommended by the 1966 Advisory Council Report,[31] would reduce public assistance's fiscal importance among the states and transfer the battles over grant levels to a normally more responsive federal arena. In view of the powerful pull of federal dollars, the matching formula might be reversed to pay the highest percent to states which combine increased tax effort with adequacy in benefit levels.

Revision and reform of state and local tax and other fiscal arrangements have long been needed for many reasons, and especially so since rising expenditures for health, housing, education, transportation, and other services, as well as for

[30] Alvin Schorr, *Poor Kids* (New York: Basic Books, 1966), Chap. 7.
[31] *Having the Power, We Have the Duty,* report of the Advisory Council on Public Welfare to the Secretary of Health, Education, and Welfare (Washington, D.C.: U.S. Government Printing Office, 1966).

public assistance, are straining financial resources while failing to meet public needs. Shifting a portion of the cost of these services, then, to personal and corporate income taxes and adopting income taxes in states which do not have them should relieve the pressure for higher levies on real and personal property and on the retail sales tax. In addition to the advantage to be gained from improved fiscal measures, a shift away from the property tax should remove public assistance as the vulnerable target of resistance to tax increases.

Other such proposals could be developed. Our major thesis, however, is that attempts to increase the political strength of our side by reducing the program's prominence for hostile interest groups constitute a useful strategy. Experience persuades us that direct confrontation mobilizes opponents of generally equal and sometimes greater strength, bringing about the "backlash" problem. Assuming that we can maintain our own interest and commitment and, while awaiting the millennium of radical change, reduce our opponents' commitment and interest; this may be the avenue to modest but progressive political success.

POSTSCRIPT

In the spring of 1969 the effect of these welfare crises upon the traditional power structure activated state governments to demand federal financial aid on a larger scale, operating through HEW and Senate leaders from the urban industrial states. The urgency of this crisis overrode the influence of state welfare directors, with state political leadership (the governors) taking the key role. We believe that during the coming decade this pressure will produce increased federal standards and assumption of federal financial responsibility for the welfare system.

If this is not successful in reducing political criticism of the welfare system, an outcome we regard as more than likely, the way may then be opened for initiating such new approaches as children's allowances, or the negative income tax.

PUBLIC WELFARE— RECOMMITTED, RESTRUCTURED, REVITALIZED

I. The Commitment

JAMES R. DUMPSON

THE 1960s HAVE WITNESSED an increasing number of attacks on public welfare. The attacks have come from all quarters—from politicians and statesmen, from public welfare administrators and staff, from social critics and theoreticians, from the communication media, from a majority of the taxpayers whose taxes support the program, and now in an organized fashion from those who have always been considered to be its direct beneficiaries. Many, if not all, of the attacks have been justified. Few of its critics, however, have searched out the underlying reasons for public welfare's deficiencies. As we consider ways to recommit, restructure, and revitalize public welfare, it is well that we understand why public welfare must be adjudged a failure in meeting effectively and satisfactorily a mission appropriate to it in the last third of the twentieth century. In some of the more recent and more thoughtful critical comments one finds that the emphasis is now less on the administration of public welfare, less on lurid exposés, and more on causative factors that lie outside the welfare system. The New York *Times*, for example, in an editorial on May 17, 1968, commenting on a statement made at a City University of New York colloquium as to one important reason behind growing public resentment against the welfare system, remarked that "Congress continues to ignore the root causes of welfare as it presses fresh attacks on the welfare system." Daniel Moynihan, in his unpublished manuscript "The Crisis in Welfare," gives a similar but more pointed reason:

Developments in the 1950s would have made it apparent to anyone closely involved that despite burgeoning prosperity, patterns of income, employment, housing, discrimination, and social services, very possibly including the welfare system itself, were somehow undermining stability of family life among the poor, particularly the urban Negro poor.

The Report of the Advisory Council on Public Welfare in its first indictment of our public welfare system declared "that the Government is, by its own standards and definitions, a major source of the poverty on which it has declared unconditional war." [1] Five years after the passage of the much heralded and, I now believe, unfortunately supported 1962 Social Security amendments, a former dean of a school of social work and a commissioner of public welfare declared the welfare system "bankrupt." And finally, in signing the infamous H.R. 12080 into law on January 2, 1968, the President of the United States in his statement added:

[1] *Having the Power, We Have the Duty,* report of the Advisory Council on Public Welfare to the Secretary of Health, Education, and Welfare (Washington, D.C.: U.S. Government Printing Office, 1966), p. xii.

"The welfare system in America is outmoded and in need of a major change." While more and more it is fashionable, politically and for us professionally, to demean public welfare administration and its personnel, there are those who focus their criticism on the systemic aspects of public welfare. We shall certainly hear more castigation of the public welfare system, and underneath this castigation, in many instances, will be revealed a deep and underlying contempt for those whom the system was designed to help. We should welcome rational, constructive criticism of a system that is unsuited to meeting human needs. But we must reject attacks, from whatever quarter, that are disguised attacks on the people the programs were designed to serve. Our first commitment is to those whom the social and economic and political systems have rejected, those who have been denied access to both power and money.

As we seek a recommitment not just to public welfare as it is, but to a restructured and revitalized public welfare system, let us not gloss over our sins of omission in not seeking basic, fundamental change. Most of us in social welfare have failed to make it clear, outside social welfare meetings and conferences, over the past two decades, that we have irrefutable evidence in the case records of every public agency that drastic change is long overdue—not only change in the public welfare system, but radical change in the social and economic systems that have brought people in ever increasing numbers to public welfare. Despite antipoverty programs and similar efforts, despite marches on Washington, despite the violence that has come to every major city in response to the violence to human dignity and self-respect by the dehumanizing experiences in the ghettos of the nation, public welfare caseloads have continued to rise because we have not as a nation got the message. The shame is that the caseloads have not risen in proportion to the need that 30 million people have experienced for decades. For the most part, we have devised policies and procedures to keep the rolls and costs down even though we knew that public welfare merely collected those whom the social and economic system rejected. There was no other place for them to go.

Federal officials are reported to have estimated that the welfare budget will increase by $100 million if the Supreme Court upholds a series of lower court decisions that will expand the rights of welfare recipients. With the outlawing of the "man-in-the-house" rule, between 200,000 and 400,000 children became qualified for welfare benefits in eighteen states. Outlawing residency laws in forty states will qualify 100,000 to 200,000 persons for public welfare benefits.[2] Whatever other reasons motivated residency and "man-in-the-house" laws and policies, they have served to deny needed assistance to children and adults at a "saving" of $100 million. What a pittance to spend for needy and underprivileged American children and their families! Our misplaced values in other areas have permitted us to spend billions that have destroyed hundreds of thousands in order, we claim, to save them. Our commitment to human wellbeing for all the people did not point out the mockery of President Lyndon B. Johnson's statement that "many in America have never had it so good." The "many" are not the 9 million Americans who depend on government handouts from public assistance. The "many" are not those mil-

[2] On April 21, 1969, the United States Supreme Court declared that it is "constitutionally impermissible" for a state to enforce a waiting period for "the purpose of inhibiting migration by needy persons into the state." The 6-to-3 decision outlaws residency laws for public welfare benefits in forty states.

lions of Americans who must live on twenty-two cents per meal per day.

Our commitment to changing the quality of life for people, for that is what I mean by a new commitment in welfare, should stimulate us to accelerate a crisis in order that the nation will be forced to seek and support alternatives to the systems that are eroding and corroding human beings. We have continued to advocate a piecemeal approach to altering the public assistance titles of the Social Security Act rather than call for a revolutionary new approach to redistributing income to deal with economic dependency and to redistributing opportunities to deal with social deprivation. We permitted ourselves to superimpose the diagnostic-treatment model of social work on the public welfare system, and so we called for more and more services without clearly defining "services" or seeking to demonstrate their relevance to dependency as we met it in public welfare. We heralded the "service amendments" that were presumably enacted to help restore people to being, in the President's terms, "taxpayers, not taxeaters." I wonder, in retrospect, as we focused primarily on the intrapsychic functioning of the poor, as we highlighted the internal causation of economic dependency rather than calling attention to and developing strategies to deal with flaws in the socioeconomic system, whether we were not really more interested in wrapping public welfare in the cloak of professional respectability than we were in human restoration. We stood by and watched the attempts to implement the 1962 amendments with their interpretation that the causes of dependency were within the individual and his need to be rehabilitated, while many words were spoken about the impact of squalid housing, the poor health services that those on public welfare could obtain, the discrimination they met in every area of living, and the depressing and immobilizing self-images that the maldistribution of opportunity produced. We watched the refusal of Congress to accompany its generous subsidies of services with mandated adequate and humane levels of financial assistance in the fifty-odd public assistance programs of the nation. We added insult to injury by promising Congress that social services would reduce welfare rolls and costs. And then we waxed content while the multisocially handicapped increased in number; those who were functionally illiterate increased; those who were discriminated against in housing, in employment, and in apprenticeship training increased; those who lived in despair, in alienation, and in powerlessness increased. And because Negroes were disproportionately represented in these increases, we heard a Presidential Commission declare that the "nation is moving toward two societies: one black, one white, separate and unequal." Public welfare, had it been living out its commitment, could have documented that finding two decades ago from the records of almost every public welfare agency. We know we have had two separate and unequal societies for years.

We need a new commitment that will no longer permit us to fail to translate our caseloads in other than statistical terms, to be defensive about caseloads that have grown from 7.5 million five years ago to 9 million today. How did the increase come about? A great majority of it reflects the separate and unequal black society of which the Kerner report [3] speaks, and also the failure of government, of industry, of social welfare, of each of us, to operationalize our

[3] *Report of the National Commission on Civil Disorders* (New York Times Co., Bantam Books, 1968), p. 1.

oft-stated commitment to national well-being through the economic and social well-being, to the security of every family, whether it is a complete or an incomplete family and irrespective of why it is incomplete, and of every individual within or outside a family. And if a social revolution is required to fulfill that commitment, let us be among the leaders.

But as we beat our breasts and murmur *"mea culpa,"* as we acknowledge the inability of public welfare as presently structured and administered to meet the needs of the poor equitably, adequately, and in dignity, I would have us understand what was said by one of the welfare rights groups in New York. Speaking of a conference that the group's board had with the Commissioner of Social Services in New York City, the editorial of its Social Work Action for Welfare Rights News Letter for May, 1968, says:

Commissioner Goldberg's remarks have a familiar ring. They represent the new "line" emerging from sincere and dedicated public servants who preside over a welfare system which requires that its beneficiaries become liars, magicians or both. He castigates the punitive programs and the existing system, claims a high degree of powerlessness, feels beholden to politicians and the state welfare department, and is always under the punitive and watchful eyes of a largely unsympathetic tax-burdened public.

These may very well be the facts of life and all concerned persons no doubt sympathize with the Commissioner's position. However, these facts cannot be used as a confessional. Why by their repetition absolve the Commissioner and his administrative staff from identifying, exposing, and correcting those ills which *are* in his jurisdiction and those within his power to change?

· · · · ·

Recipients cannot wait for microscopic public welfare changes. Improvements are needed now, and are possible now.

As we think of a recommitment in public welfare, we need to take these words quite seriously. Radical change is required in the welfare system, and if we do not join in providing the leadership for it, it will be done in spite of us. Will we make that commitment? When candidates for public office vie for support and votes and fall over each other attesting to the inadequacy, the inappropriateness, the bankruptcy of public welfare, we need to quote these words to them, supported by our experiences of frustration and futility in attempting to make a public welfare system designed in concept and practice to meet the situation and needs of a quarter of a century and more ago, meet the needs of 30 million poor people now and in the years immediately ahead.

As we contemplate our commitment and as we attempt to envision what must be the public welfare program for tomorrow, I suggest that we accept that government has the ultimate responsibility to assure that human need is appropriately satisfied. We must be certain that our new understanding of the interventive role of government in altering the systems that affect people's well-being, and our new perception of peoples' right to have a part in the determination of the nature and content of the intervention are reflected in our commitment. We must identify the alternatives and consequences of what the restructured and revitalized system must provide—once we are through, and help others to be through, with the confession of past error and the absolution for having been either deaf to, or remiss in responding to, the needs of people.

I believe that we Americans need to be reminded again and again of the ultimate function of our government. We created and continue to support this government of ours for

the good of all of us. Through our government, we are committed to promoting, safeguarding, and guaranteeing the
human rights of every individual and the opportunities for
assuming responsibilities that are inherent in our conviction
about the dignity and essential worth of every individual.
This conviction is the very embracement of our Judeo-
Christian heritage. If we accept this as our fundamental
premise for the existence of the government of these United
States, then the responsibilities which it carries are clear,
specific, and inescapable. All actions of government must be
directed to the common good. But that government is not a
vague, shadowy specter; it does not fit into an "it-and-we"
formulation; it is not any one person or any group of persons. It is each one of us. This is the philosophy of democracy in government of, by, and for *all* of its people. It is
within this context that I find meaning to the phrase "commitment to *public* welfare."

Just as we as a nation must yet learn fully how to exercise
this philosophy of government, of people acting together for
the good of people, so must public welfare function because
of and within this philosophy. Public welfare is an important, indeed an inescapable, expression of our commitment
to human well-being: not to some individuals whose
color or accent of language we consider acceptable; not excluding those who by the accident of birth are classified as
illegitimate and therefore "undeserving"; not excluding
those who are strangers or who are not "our kind" or who
"belong" elsewhere. Commitment to the primacy of human
values and of government as the guardian of those values
demands that public welfare, government's expression of
our national conscience, accept human need as the sole
criterion for the limits of its concern and responsibility.

Then and only then will public welfare be one with government, actively and aggressively working for all the people. On this philosophical base must rest public policy goals, legislative mandates, and the administration of public welfare. The economic, social, and moral well-being of the nation depends on the extent and the quality of our effort to assure the human rights of each individual—black and white, in Mississippi and in California; young and old—his individual well-being, and the fullest opportunity possible for him to carry his share of responsibility for the common good. Toward this end, public welfare must play a crucial role.

There are few, I believe, who will disagree with these somewhat broad, philosophical statements. Most Americans, at whatever position in the political spectrum they stand, will say that they have no problem with this position. They all can join in such a commitment to public welfare as broadly defined.

It is when this philosophical position must be translated into legislation, agency policies, and administrative practices that the rub comes. It is then that such terms as "tax-eaters," "undeserving," are acceptable when applied to needy people. It is then that the association of welfare with Negroes and other racial or cultural minorities causes the flak, the public resentment and the white backlash that underlies much of that public resentment about public welfare, and, subtly, the disdain and contempt with which many of our staffs and associates hold the poor. It is then that the association of welfare is made with immorality, with sin, if you will, and provides a basis for rejection not only of "the immoral" and "the sinful" but of the program that dares to support them. When we succeed in associating Negroes and other minorities and sex and dependency in a

formulation of causal relationships, then our philosophical
stance about the role of government in meeting human
need runs into serious trouble. We must recognize that these
relationships have been deliberately contrived. We need to
be sure for what purpose and by whom. Can we make a
new commitment to a restructured, revitalized public welfare that has its roots in the concept of government that I
have stated without dealing frankly and honestly with our
feelings about "all sorts and conditions of men"? I doubt it.
I suggest that we begin with our own feelings about financial dependency, about ethnic and cultural difference, about
value difference.

Further, I maintain that our perception of government in
action, the newly emerging relationship among its service levels and our new insights about people, particularly people
in need, may create difficulty for many of us in making the
new commitment that the program planners would have us
make.

I sense a growing, albeit reluctant, acceptance and a broad-
ening but snail's-pace implementation of the position that
government must utilize all of its resources—social, economic, and political—for the realization of human well-
being. For me this is the ultimate goal of a democratic society, and its government thereby assumes ultimate responsibility for what happens to all of its people. If my observation is correct, then the possibilities and alternatives available to government for human well-being are enormously
enlarged. Public welfare may very well, as I hope it will,
shift its primary emphasis to the provision of a broad range
of social services without reference to any income-test or
means-test mechanisms. We may be able, as I hope we will,
to broaden further the use of general tax funds not only to
support a truly residual public assistance program at a level

in keeping with American values and standards in every county and state and American possession, but to support a children's or family allowance with a realistic monthly payment for every child solely because he is a child, and to put material substance behind our oft-stated commitment to the importance of our children and the social and economic dividends of strengthening family life in our nation. The public welfare system to which we are being asked to make a new commitment is not the patched-up, overamended system of 1935. If increased government intervention in behalf of people who need that intervention and our economic and political resources are so utilized, we shall be able to remove the barriers to achieving our national goal for people. Public welfare as one of government's instruments in implementing that goal will strip itself of those dehumanizing aspects which in part have been perpetuated for financial reasons.

I believe that as a nation we are achieving not only a new perception of responsibility but of people in need—of those we seek to serve and also of ourselves as the helpers. Painfully for many of us, to be sure, resistantly for others, we are coming to accept that those who are the consumers of our services, those who are the targets of our efforts, must be involved in the development and administration of those services and efforts. We are learning that we do not always know what is best for individuals and families; that we were in great error when we thought or behaved in practice as if those in need had little to contribute to the solution of their own or any other social problems. Our deeper understanding of the great potentials of our most deprived and underprivileged, our recognition of the untapped resources in creativity and the ability to be self-directing, underscores the validity of the principle of maximum feasible participation of the consumer of our services. Public welfare, not un-like every other human endeavor, must find ways to in-corporate this principle into its structure and practices; must find ways to involve those it serves as collaborators, whatever their color, whatever their style of life, and regard-less of how we have forced them to adjust to or to compro-mise the values we consider dominant. Indeed, as we strengthen this conviction about the worth and potential of people who have known rejection and deprivation, a new model for administering public welfare, as other social wel-fare programs, should be considered, one that places major administrative responsibility in the hands of those for whom the programs and services are designed. If people in the neighborhoods should control their public schools, as many in New York City advocate, then people in the neigh-borhoods should control and administer other public serv-ices. Public welfare will be called on every day to find ways to accommodate its administration to this changed percep-tion of the users of its services. A new commitment to public welfare will require our individual commitment to this essential expression of human dignity and self-respect.

The Technical Assistance Project of the American Public Welfare Association reports on the testimony in March, 1967, of Richard Boone, Executive Director of the Citizen's Crusade against Poverty, before the public hearings of the Senate Subcommittee on Labor and Poverty. In that testi-mony Mr. Boone specified "three guiding principles against which all poverty related programs should be measured:

1. *Economic Security:* What is the impact of a particular pro-gram on providing economic security for a poor person and his family?
2. *Freedom:* What impact does the program have in protecting

and promoting freedom for the persons affected and their power to have alternatives and make choices in all areas of fundamental human concern?

3. *Responsibility:* How does the program provide opportunities for persons involved to make effective contributions to their families, to communities, and for the common good? Are they just consumers? Or do we offer them opportunities to be producers for the good of their communities and the Nation? [4]

Stated in other terms, the criteria against all public welfare programs may be measured to meet a viable realistic social policy goal for Americans in this last third of the twentieth century are:

1. *Adequacy:* a guarantee of income sufficient to provide for every person a level of living in accordance with American standards of physical and mental health and over-all social well-being

2. *Certainty or social guarantee:* the availability of the income and social supports as a matter of right, a minimum of subjective, administrative judgment, and fully and promptly available without interruption

3. *Equity:* assurance that all families in similar circumstances receive the same treatment without reference to the ability or willingness of a state or local jurisdiction to provide the assistance and social supports

4. *Dignity:* assurance that the beneficiaries have all the rights and privileges of other citizens and no greater and no less responsibility for observing the laws of the land.

Whether we accept Boone's triad of economic security, freedom, and responsibility, or the oft-quoted quartet of ad-

4 Technical Assistance Project, American Public Welfare Association, *Goals, Commitments, Barriers, Propositions—Challenge to Validity* (Chicago: the Association, 1967; mimeographed), p. 3.

equacy, certainty, equity, and dignity, we are compelled to state that public welfare fails to meet these criteria. Our commitment for a restructured and revitalized public welfare system is predicated on some basic changes in the American systems—change in the system by which we effect distribution of the nation's income, change in the system by which we deliver the services and social supports required by all of us for the realization of our potential and for the enrichment of the quality of living for all in our land. Income and services and other social supports must be accompanied by a change in the distribution of power from the relatively few to all Americans and by a change in the physical environment that makes possible a constructive use of the income and the power. All of public welfare's policies, programs, and accomplishments must reflect these goals and be one of American Society's instruments for their realization.

As one reviews these proposed commitments of public welfare, one surely must sense that underlying all of them is a thrust for adequate income, services, and supports for all of us toward the end that the freedom and dignity of those who are poor may be enhanced, but equally so that the freedom and dignity of all Americans may be enhanced. Until the poor are secure and free and live in dignity no American can be secure and free and live in freedom. Surely this message came through loudly and clearly in the Kerner report.[5] As one reads the report and ponders its findings in Part I—"What Happened?"—through Part II—"Why Did It Happen?"—the role of a recommitted, restructured, and revitalized public welfare becomes quite clear. I was not surprised, then, to find in Part III—"What Can Be Done"—

5 *Op. cit.*

among the recommendations for national action a section on public welfare. The contribution of public welfare to the scorching indictment of the report cannot be overlooked. By its policies and procedures, its entire administrative thrust, public welfare has helped support "two societies, one black, one white—separate and unequal." We need only read the two critical deficiencies of public welfare set forth in the Kerner report. They are but a summation of all we have known and refused or failed to change. The Commission's recommendations to the federal government, acting with state and local governments, and relying on the ultimate responsibility of government for what happens to people, are a summation of the recommendations that are "old hat" to all of us who have expressed concern about the viability of public welfare in the 1960s and the years ahead.

Why do I turn now to the Kerner report? It seems to me that if we do not deal swiftly with the ingredients of the racism that the report states is responsible for the urban crisis of which the welfare crisis is but a part, any future discussion of recommitment, restructuring, or revitalizing public welfare or any other of our outmoded institutions will be useless.

As I told a conference of the Child Welfare League, we have had revealed to us the awful chasm between what we believe about people, blacks and whites, and what we do in behalf of people, blacks and whites; a chasm between our dream for our nation and what we allocate of our resources and energies in order to fulfill that dream. I was once told that the first thing to do to make a dream come true is to wake up. Too many Americans have yet to wake up. Many of us in social welfare are still thinking and behaving in a "business-as-usual" manner. Events have told us for a long time that we can no longer be satisfied with progress measured in inches, by a few excellent amendments to the Social Security Act that increased benefits and increased authorizations for child welfare services, by experiments to test simplification, or alternative income mechanisms. There is a crisis in public welfare caused by our failure to put first things first, to examine and redefine what we are doing, what we should do, what we can do *now* to deal effectively with the crisis that sees 30 million Americans still economically and socially consigned to poverty and deprivation.

Some years ago, the stability and security of the nation were in jeopardy. What did we do? We went to war—total war. As a nation we mobilized all of our resources to protect and defend our stability and security. The stability and security of the nation are in jeopardy today, but not from without. Another total mobilization is required of all our resources, including the knowledge, skill, and understanding of social welfare, which is one of the nation's unique resources. We need to determine how we can contribute to obtaining and maintaining a single, integrated society. We need to find out how we can engage in a war against prejudice and its manifestations in jobs, income, education, and housing. We need to find out how we can listen more carefully to those poor whom we serve and understand from them what they want and how we can help them get it. We need to ask what is our role as a profession and as individuals in achieving social justice and the security and well-being of *all* of our people. And we need to look not only at things as they are and ask why, but in Shaw's phrase, "dream things that never were and ask why not."

I am urging that we face honestly and fearlessly the top agenda item of our national experience—racism and the resultant urban and welfare crises; that we define our role as a profession and as individuals in relation to these crises, and to social action; that as professionals and as agencies we determine in what ways we must change, how we must reorder the priorities of our concern, reallocate our energies, time, and resources to discover strategies for increasing our contribution to deal with the critical issues of race and security, and peace in our time. The time for "business as usual" as social workers, as agencies, and as citizens is at an end. And if for some of us this means fewer luxuries and wounded pride, an honest confession, a new commitment, so must it be.

In the words again of the Kerner report:

It is time now to turn with all the purpose at our command to the major unfinished business of this nation. It is time to adopt strategies for action that will produce quick and visible progress. It is time to make good the promises of American democracy to all citizens—urban and rural, white and black, Spanish-surname, American Indian, and every minority group. . . . It is time now to end the destruction and the violence, not only in the streets of the ghetto but in the lives of people.[6]

II. The Problem
NORMAN V. LOURIE

WE AND A FEW ALLIES HAVE FOUGHT vigorously against destitution and poverty in our own style for many years. Now we are not so alone, and some new styles have been developed in this battle.

[6] *Ibid.*

One would be extremely unobservant if he did not notice the turbulence of these times. There can be no question that this turbulence is generated by a feeling that though we have accomplished a great deal, it is not enough.

Possibly we would be a great deal more concerned if the turbulence were being evidenced at some other point in history. My optimism is maintained by the number of forward strides we have made through the President's Commission on Civil Disorders, the war on poverty, and the Presidential Commission on Income Maintenance. One of the most hopeful signs of our time is the ability of our citizenry to articulate their requirements from government and to induce change. Resurrection City [1] was dramatic evidence that the American poor, no longer complacent, are taking a hand in their own rehabilitation. The black power movements are healthy attempts to replace discrimination against minorities with status and dignity; to replace the major mental health problem of racism with equal citizenship. Students are reminding us that the generation gap exists. In June, 1968, the Supreme Court outlawed the man-in-the-house rules in public assistance, and there are hopeful signs that the residence requirement may be eliminated. There are legal stirrings to establish reasonable assistance levels as a right.

The turmoil in the land continues to remind us that we are far from achieving the goal and completing the mission. Poverty, which this wealthy nation is morally obligated to solve, is still among us. We must develop a national commitment to children, to relieve their suffering and poverty.

From the bottom—from the people, in the best expres-

[1] A tent city created in Washington, D.C., in the spring of 1968 by poor people from over the country—a "sit-in" between the Washington and Lincoln monuments.

sion of the traditional American way—and from the top—
political, bureaucratic, and upper-strata groups—a new national policy is emerging. We appear more ready to take
full responsibility for the well-being and the livelihood of
the destitute and the poverty-stricken.

This is the basis for encouragement. This is the point
from which public welfare must recommit itself, restructure
and revitalize, if it is to continue to be a force for good.

Philip Klein dedicates his recent book to "the unsung toil-
ers in the rank and file of public assistance services who
navigate a precarious course between the ill-served client
and regimented bureaucracy under the stern eye of the reluctant taxpayer." [2] The reluctant taxpayer is becoming less
reluctant on the question of a guaranteed minimum
income.[3] The ill-served client is learning how to take his
place as a dignified citizen with political "clout." The regimented bureaucrats, who sometimes shout that our "system
is bankrupt," are becoming freed to create a less severe system which can better serve to close the gap between promise
and performance.

The American Public Welfare Association (APWA), particularly through its Technical Assistance Project, is giving
us leadership and showing the way. The project is devoted
to helping public welfare agencies retool for the new day
and the new opportunities.

The first publication of the project, *Goals, Commitments,
Barriers, Propositions—Challenge to Validity,* made the issues very clear.

[2] Philip Klein, *From Philanthropy to Social Welfare: an American
Cultural Perspective* (San Francisco: Jossey-Bass, Inc., 1968), p. x.
[3] A recent Gallup Poll revealed that more Americans than not, were
favorable to the guaranteed income idea.

The only honest thing for "regimented bureaucrats" to do is to recognize that the chains that bind us are the same chains that bind the destitute and the poverty-stricken; that there is considerable invalidity in our methods and structures; and that as the chains are unbound we should leap forward to seek better, more valid ways.

The Advisory Council on Public Welfare found public welfare programs short on several counts. They are not: available to all they are intended to protect; adequate to meet their needs; consistent with the standards of the society in which they live; or available on a dignified basis as a matter of legal right. Public welfare was itself found to be a "major source of poverty." [4]

No one today questions that an economic maintenance program is number one on the agenda. Our task is to support the efforts to achieve it. Meantime, the present public assistance system needs massive improvement. Grant levels must be brought up to culturally accepted and realistic standards. We have tried everything else. Now we must try money.

State levels of assistance will not be brought up to standard until there are federal mandates for grant levels and standards of living. I believe that the federal government should pay more of the cash grant share—perhaps 100 percent, including general assistance. There should be one criterion—need—and no categories. This is a political issue, and we have substantial evidence that ultimately Congress will do what the people wish.

Putting it simply, relief of destitution and poverty means

4 *Having the Power, We Have the Duty*, report of the Advisory Council on Public Welfare to the Secretary of Health, Education, and Welfare (Washington, D.C.: U.S. Government Printing Office, 1966).

making sure that people have enough money. That is what Resurrection City was about, and for many of its residents the answer was a job. This is the first task. We have to support the poor people's movements just as we expect those movements to support our legislative objectives. They are unalterably intertwined. There have been many suggestions for new guaranteed minimum income schemes. I submit that an enlightened public assistance system is in effect a guaranteed minimum income scheme. In fact, no proposed scheme (except that for the children's allowance, which I approve because it goes to all children and represents a national commitment to children) can avoid a means test. Even the proposed negative income tax is based on the principle of a means test. It would still require an assistance-like system to deal with emergencies. Why have two means test systems? I believe that if we corrected all the negatives in public assistance, it and the negative income tax would be very much alike. The decision as to whether the system should be administered by the Internal Revenue Service or by HEW would be a political one.

Mary Switzer, Administrator of the Social and Rehabilitation Administration, and Wilbur Cohen, former Secretary of the Department of Health, Education, and Welfare (HEW), have both made it clear that in administering the Social Security Act, as amended in 1967, they were following a policy of separating the giving of assistance from the giving of services. Effective July 1, 1968, HEW has also made it mandatory that the states shall begin to install a declaration system.

Elementary enough in concept, separation, from the standpoint of operations, means several things. The Technical Assistance Project document puts it in clear terms:

Major systemic aspects of the structure and process of public welfare as it is today tend to dehumanize those in need whether they be clients or those technically ineligible. These dehumanizing features include:

The investigations

The restrictive eligibility requirements

The delay in receiving assistance

The unrealistic "standard of need"

The use of long-obsolete price schedules in computing the "budgeted" needs

The confiscation of resources and the resultant destruction of incentives essential to sustain self-effort

The inaccessibility of the appeals process and the time lags and formalities inherent in using it and unfairness in having decisions reviewed by those who made them initially

The awesome power gap between client and caseworker and the forces within the system that provide temptations to misuse the power to withhold or to compel

The established policy of dealing with clients in isolation from representatives of their organizations or from legal counsel, increases their sense of helplessness and alienation

The passive, helpless, insecure, childlike role assigned to the client by the welfare agency that intensifies his despair and alienation

The exclusion of representatives of the clients or of the community of the poor from participation in the development or appraisal of the policies that apply to them

The dubious practice of relying primarily on inadequately trained "caseworkers" to serve a population many of whose problems are clearly related to a very deprived physical and social environment and a stunted opportunity structure

The lack of truly rehabilitative services

The inaccessibility of offices and personnel

The lack of legal help in civil matters including relationships with the welfare system

The striking absence of any organized, consistent program to inform the clients and the community of the poor of the benefits and services which the welfare department is supposed to provide

The prevalent lack of active accommodation of welfare operations to common efforts with other public and private welfare agencies or with organizations of the poor to solve common problems and achieve common goals.[5]

These must go. These must be corrected.

The APWA project report then goes on to state a series of propositions which are avenues by which the effectiveness of public welfare could be significantly increased as a positive and acceptable force in the lives of the poor:

1. Expanding and improving the various means of communication, mutual understanding and involvement of recipients and other poor people
2. Instituting processes which recognize the rights of recipient citizens to privacy and control over their personal affairs and provide positive protections for the exercise of those rights which are essential to the well-being of all citizens
3. Eliminating the infringements and limitations on personal privacy, choice and achievement inherent in the prevalent system of applying for assistance or service with attendant investigation procedures
4. Reformulating goals and policies for the treatment of earnings, contributions from relatives, or other income, in terms of their impact on clients' lives
5. Reconstructing the components of service activities, bringing into better focus and visibility, both the immediate and long-term purposes they serve, and the means by which these are obtained.[6]

In Pennsylvania we made a firm and conclusive decision to give higher public assistance grants the first priority and we mandated that eligibility be separated from services in all counties. On February 1, 1968, we separated them in four

[5] Technical Assistance Project, American Public Welfare Association, *Goals, Commitments, Barriers, Propositions—Challenge to Validity* (Chicago: the Association, 1967), pp. 9–10.

[6] *Ibid.,* p. 16.

counties as the first step to complete separation in all sixty-seven counties. Using a declaration system administered by noncollege-graduate eligibility technicians, we started with unsophisticated sampling techniques to determine the validity of our method. We intend to refine the method and have embarked on a contracted exhaustive systems study of the entire eligibility process. This will doubtless result in a computer-based arrangement for maximum simplification and in a sophisticated information system. Thirty-three counties now have programs separated.

We have encouraged and, indeed, lent staff effort to the civic education of client groups, and our administrators are directed to open channels of communication to organized representatives of program participants. Plans are under way to expand this participation into policy-making levels.

The Governor has asked the legislature to increase grants by 30 percent to bring them closer to our full cost-of-living standard. In our next budget we plan to go to 100 percent of an updated cost-of-living standard.

In several other states too, experimentation is going on to separate services from eligibility.

This must be the immediate direction of social welfare's grant program while we and our new allies seek a more adequate money-giving arrangement. "Guaranteed minimum income" will be a slogan until a tested, administerable, new system is agreed upon and developed.

We know that a massive shift of vast numbers of the aged, the disabled, and the blind to the social insurance system will reduce public assistance rolls. We know, too, that this change has to be pursued in the political arena.

We know that such programs as that of the model cities

give us the opportunity to experiment with guaranteed minimum income schemes. It is encouraging to note the experiments undertaken at the University of Wisconsin and by Mathematica, Inc., in New Jersey, to test guaranteed minimum income devices. We need more of this.

It must be reemphasized that improving the public assistance system is not simply a matter of separating eligibility, installing a declaration system, and increasing grants. Incentives must be built in because we also have a series of positive motives. For those with the capacity and the desire for work, we seek productive jobs at a living wage. An adequate, dignified system of providing income for those who cannot or should not work is the counterpart.

Here again the APWA Technical Assistance Project gives us some guidelines as to what public assistance must do to render itself a guaranteed minimum income system.

1. Developing and using a standard of "need" based on the "poverty-line" concept or some modification of it, using family-size variables, or on customary and common low-income expenditure patterns
2. Distinguishing between "standard of need" applying to persons and "standards of aid" as conditioned by agency limitations
3. Exempting income from all sources which together with the aid to which the recipient is otherwise entitled does not exceed the "standard of need," and consideration above this level of only a percentage, increasing as the amount increases
4. Exempting owned homes, and other property up to a value equivalent to some multiple of the annual "standard of need"
5. Eliminating most special needs from grant consideration and providing them as an element in the service to which they are related—either as a direct function performed by employees, or as an element in the cost of purchased service.[7]

7 *Ibid.*, p. 19.

HEW has also directed the states to use program participants as employees and as policy advisers, and federal civil service restrictions have been revised to help us with employment matters. Many public welfare agencies have already moved in this direction to:

1. Use recipients or other residents of the neighborhoods to help prepare and distribute simple written information about what is available, who is entitled to it, and how to get it
2. Employ recipients or residents of poorer neighborhoods as community aides
3. Employ and train recipients or members of the poorer communities as case aides or members of service units
4. Redeploy staff and offices to establish contact points in the neighborhoods where the poor are concentrated
5. Encourage organizations of recipients who are strong enough to represent themselves
6. Encourage community aides and other leaders to represent the interests of individuals
7. Develop methods of carrying on a dialogue between administrative heads of departments and organizations of the poor for response to questions and complaints and for interpretation of needs
8. Encourage participation of recipients and other poor people in hearings and on study and advisory committees
9. Seek consultation with, and reaction from, recipients and other poor people about proposed policies and programs.

In regard to service there are equally serious restructuring and revitalizing tasks to be accomplished. In general, we can say that we must improve the focus, level, and productivity of our service resources. The federal reorganization allows services to be better patterned, more coherent, and more visible. The 1967 amendments broadened the possibilities for using previously unavailable resources through purchase and contract.

In Pennsylvania we have, as part of the separation process, embarked on new approaches to service. The 1962 amendments gave us many opportunities which we did not utilize sufficiently. When used, they produced results.

Pennsylvania has developed combination family service-settlement house programs in public housing projects. Like other states, Pennsylvania has opened outreach centers. Some states, like California and Pennsylvania, have used public welfare personnel to carry a degree of aftercare responsibility for former mental institution patients. Pennsylvania has opened a series of Governor's branch offices where people may bring their problems for referral to other, mostly public, services. It has a reporting system which gives the state Administration information on need and acts as a monitoring device on the quality of response by all state human service agencies. The 1962 amendments spurred day care development.

No state, however, has achieved an ideal structuring of social services. There are many gaps; there are fragmented and uncoordinated operations. Public welfare service operations have been maintained as a subordinate responsibility, commanding attention only as time and effort were available by staff primarily responsible for eligibility determination. This has prevented us from attacking the issue, organizing and providing services clearly defined in relation to goal, function, or method, targeted on a priority basis to known populations, with clearly defined products and tested by evaluation and cost-effectiveness studies.

We talk glibly about coordination, but in practice it has been for the most part a myth. There has been little effective coordination of resources within public departments, within public agencies, or among public agencies, voluntary agencies, and the private sector, including business and industry.

The list of potential services can be as unlimited as the range of human need and desire: employment and work training; child and adult welfare, including foster care, day care, and homemaker services; family planning, counseling, leisure-time services, and family life education; education in home and financial management; a wide range of monitored health care; legal services; and a wide range of advocacy services designed to help people get benefits.

If we mean to express our new national policy in a rational service delivery system, we have to go beyond conceiving of social welfare as a series of loosely connected agencies and institutions. If welfare as a set of services is to be replaced by welfare as a policy to assure the well-being of all the people, the implications lead not only to Alfred Kahn's concept of social utilities but to the concept of creating a system which includes methodology and machinery which can prescribe service, requisition service, and ensure service.

We need not only a social engineering effort. We need an ecumenical movement. Our pluralistic system with its multiple, overlapping laws, programs, and money streams creates almost insuperable barriers to establishing a rational system.

To achieve this condition is not easy because we have multiproblems to tackle. The single-problem systems, whatever their internal guild difficulties, have been able to get at problems more logically, at least in the public sector. A community has only one educational system and one police system, for instance. In the social welfare and health fields the overlapping, fragmentation, and competition are extensive.

We have many barriers, a wide variety of competitive forces. We are not geared to a social utility approach. While we agree that all the human service problems are interrelated, our reservoirs spill into one another and our pipes seldom connect, and when they do, the joints are not well welded. People and their problems lie in the gaps between. The process of refer and transfer, pull and haul, is wearing and relatively unproductive. We do not prescribe and requisition services, which would be proper procedure if the system were tight.

It is encouraging to see us getting back to the neighborhoods, where settlement workers used to give multiphasic services. But it is discouraging to see several units in HEW, the Office of Economic Opportunity, and the Department of Housing and Urban Development opening comprehensive neighborhood centers which, like the traditional programs, compete for the consumer. In the desire of each one to be the comprehensive service delivery agent, we risk incomprehensible comprehensiveness. It would seem that in reaction to past institutional insufficiencies we are fragmenting services even more.

I am not so naïve as to propose a Department of Everything but I do propose that we believe that human service needs are interrelated. We had best restructure and retool so that we may deal with the whole man rather than just talk about him; that we may deal with whole problems rather than with pieces, with symptoms.

The ultimate answer is quite clear. It is not enough to in-
undate, to saturate the community with services. People,
because of habit, life style, placement of services or the ways
in which they are offered, can be overlooked. Studies of sat-
urated service arrangements have proved this. For instance,
in meeting the needs of children, the most satisfying solution although it may be, for now, impractical, would be for
each conception and each birth to be noted and monitored
to insure that each pregnant woman and each child would
get everything we have to offer that might minimize the
risks for that child.

I have no one final solution to offer. In Pennsylvania,
however, as we go about separating and restructuring, we
are following principles which we hope may eliminate some
of the characteristics of social welfare systems which must be
overcome if we are to make coordination more than a myth.

1. There should be the same area boundaries for planning and for priority development of related programs. Effective July 1, 1968, the Governor has directed all state
human services agencies to operate within designated re-
gional geographical boundaries.

2. The same machinery should be used for data collection, analysis, and evaluation. Pennsylvania is approaching
this and is in the process of installing a modern information
system for our grant program. We are on the way to doing
the same for our service program. We will one day be in a
position to approach other programs both within and outside our department to talk about data communication between programs.

3. At the state level, there should be strong integrating
machinery to mandate communication between programs
and to assist the Governor in priority development and de-

cision-making. In the Governor's office we have a well-staffed, cabinet-level Council for Human Services which is a communication and planning instrument.

While almost every agency that functions at the local level feels that it has the qualifications to be the coordinator, teacher, monitor, and social utilities commission type of instrument, only one can emerge in this role ultimately. Because it is present in every county, because of its philosophical, fiscal, and personnel base, I believe that public welfare, if it retools and restructures, has a logical claim to this role. It is not prepared now, but we hope that it will be. Its clientele includes the widest range of vulnerable people. It has broad experience, but first it will have to change its own style and image.

The approaches I suggest, which undergird our efforts in Pennsylvania, are not new, and I have stated them on a number of occasions. No principle is more important than ease of accessibility to service. No principle is more important than that our approach to service be a vigorous outreach with strong components of advocacy, involvement of participants in policy, and insistence that we help people to know what are their benefits.

Within these principles, there is need for a system of problem classification and assignment of responsibility that all segments in one agency can use. It would be ideal if all agencies would use the same system. The objectives of such a system would be to provide:

1. A clear basis for quickly determining service needs, for making a plan for requisition of services necessary to fulfill the plan, and for planning evaluation of the results by means of constant monitoring of the process

2. Improved communication between all personnel and disciplines in the same agency and among agencies
3. Early recognition of disorders in individuals and families, followed by preventive intervention on the public health model
4. Collection of comparable data on all, or a sample of, cases in the agency and across agency lines for agency, interagency, and community-wide action and for epidemiological and planning studies
5. Better utilization of manpower at all skill levels for rehabilitative purposes
6. Better information for use in planning controlled studies of specific treatment of specific disorders or of contributing societal conditions as well as for providing a better base line for evaluation studies.

At the outset, in our separation process, we offer each cash recipient a choice of service, unless a social study is required. We are experimenting with long- and short-term service units and we visualize a service system which will be open to noncash-grant clientele as freely as to those who receive grants. We recognize the need for a sophisticated service accounting system and for a great deal more knowledge than we now have about service, relevance, delivery, and structuring. We are engaged in major studies in these fields, using the technical assistance machinery of the APWA as our contractor. They are, at the same time, designing a total service system for us.

Aside from our own restructuring, we know that there will need to be changes in other agency structures either to create new agencies or facilities or to eliminate some and consolidate others. This will require considerable statesmanship at all levels of bureaucratic, political, and legislative power. We shall be encouraged in these efforts by the interests newly visible in the people we serve as well as in the general community.

Traditionally, community leadership and power are diffuse. Most communities suffer from unwillingness to ascribe leadership and follow it. Everyone believes in coordination —if he can be the coordinator. There can be no coordination without subordination. This means integration under one directive force. I think we need the stronger concept and that we must reach for it.

We will need many changes in agency policy and function. Many interests will have to give way in order to achieve the interagency arrangements and agreements necessary to assume the flow of problems from intake to acceptance and requisition, through evaluation, treatment, and reporting. Such a continuous flow is seldom present now.

Unless such systematic approaches are developed, we shall have many things, but they will be neither planned nor comprehensive. Many activities are carried out in the name of planning which are not really planning. They may be educational, communicative, cooperative, and so on, but they are not planning.

While no particular mode of structure and organization of services guarantees, by itself, either quality or coverage, most of our agencies are known to be presently incomplete and inadequate to the task. I suggest that we should be free enough to renovate the old and, if necessary, to create new structures, to give up old ways for the greater good.

While we do not possess all the knowledge about the dimensions of need or of treatment method, we know where to look. We have to be bold enough, then, to try new ways.

The provision of sufficient money for those who cannot be expected to earn it is a clear enough mandate.

The scope and nature of social services are more complex, to be determined by our culture and by what society wishes to prescribe. Since we profess total compassion, then we need wisdom, common sense, and devotion to task.

I see the promise of a national policy which will allow a modern, mature social welfare system. We have the technical competence. Organization and structure can be inhibitors or expediters. Wise leaders will know how to use them well and how to make them the agents for all of the people.

THE LONG ROAD
FROM COMMITMENT TO
ACCOMPLISHMENT

BETTY L. PRESLEY AND HELEN E. KEE

PERHAPS EVEN IN 1967 A DISCUSSION OF separation of eligibility and money payment services from social services within the public welfare system would have been considered innovative, if not daring. Today federal policy strongly supports such a separation of functions. Many states already have begun, or are planning to make, staffing changes preparatory to the separation of these functions. In some cases the states have planned the steps to be taken. Other jurisdictions appear to be jumping on the band wagon without careful thought to the implications of the change at the practice level.

We consider the separation of money payments from social services within the public welfare system to be a palliative, stop-gap action between today's tradition-laden public welfare structure and tomorrow's money-payment system under Social Security or, if necessary, under a separate in-

come-maintenance system. Before many more years, we believe, money payments based on need alone will have become a reality. The public, both tax-paying and recipient,
will not and should not continue to accept today's anach-
ronistic public welfare system. One question that should be
faced now, in preparation for this inevitable change, is what
should happen to public social services. What is their function? What should their role be? Should they continue in a
public department at all?

We must confront some of our own stated convictions
and the reservations that impede their full implementation.
We must face these objections if we are to provide efficiently
and effectively public social services that are relevant and
significant. We are "on the spot." When social work staff is
not responsible for eligibility and money payments, it will
no longer be possible for us to say that "if only we had less
paper work we could do more." We must find out what that
"more" is and how effective we can be in doing what we say
we have always wanted to be free to do.

Marin County, California, is in the fourteenth year of
a local public policy committed to adequate social services
aimed at economic and/or personal rehabilitation and the
protection of people. This policy preceded the 1956 Social
Security amendments, stating that public welfare should
provide services to strengthen family life and promote maximum self-support and self-care of public welfare recipients.
The 1962 amendments mandated these services and supported the mandate with funds.

Unfortunately, the service objectives were incorporated
into a superstructure which had evolved to administer cate-
gorical money payments. The mandated service objectives
were intended to produce results, but the prescribed stan-

dards established service dosages which frustrated the objectives. The good intentions were violated. Expectations have been high, and production disappointing. The rapid expansion of social legislation, the increased cost, the social worker manpower shortage, and the changing society around us force a reexamination of the traditional structures. The problem is not just one of money and manpower; it concerns the appropriate use of both under conditions which will produce results. We must get out of our traditional ruts and take a look at objectives and at our place in accomplishing those objectives.

A reexamination of the legislative base of public welfare reveals some directives obscured by traditional practice. A gap, if not a chasm, exists between "word" and "deed." This discussion will do a little soul searching on just four of these statements of principle:

1. Applicants for public assistance who meet legally established eligibility requirements are entitled to public funds in an amount set by law, without undue delay, unnecessary procedures, or harassment.

2. Applicants for public assistance are capable, willing, and should be depended upon to participate fully in establishing their own eligibility.

3. Public welfare agencies are mandated to provide services to strengthen, rehabilitate, and protect families and individuals who are or may become economically or socially dependent.

4. The public has a right to expect social services to be provided, but the granting of money is not a license for public agency staff to intervene in all facets of individual or family functioning. The recipient may refuse all social services or select that service which he finds useful to him.

(The only exceptions to this refusal right are court-adjudi-
cated protective services.)

The precepts expressed in the first two statements, the
right of eligible persons to receive a money payment and
the responsibility of the applicant to participate fully in establishing his own eligibility, lead directly to the conclusion
that a self-administered declaration of eligibility can and
should be instituted. Most applicants are literate and have
had experience in filling out job applications and tax reports. Those who cannot do so themselves have other means
of completing the papers necessary in our paper-oriented
world. A departmental staff member can assist if relatives,
friends, or other resource persons are not available. We
must ask ourselves why we think there should be any difficulty when a person applies for public assistance. Cannot an
individual capable of verbalizing facts write these same facts
on an appropriately designed form? Are our present methods wasting staff time as well as underrating the applicant's
ability? Is the spoken word more reliable than the written
word? I doubt it. In fact, there is some indication in our experience that the opposite may be true.

A second conclusion might be drawn from the first two
precepts. Eligibility requirements and money grants are or
should be based on facts clearly defined to identify public
responsibility and to protect the rights of persons eligible to
receive assistance. Processing of the data received can be
done by persons trained to know and apply the criteria. It
should not require a master's degree in social work or even
an undergraduate social work major to apply the criteria to
the facts. We have said for years that the paper work associated with money payment wastes trained social service
manpower. Yet, faced with the opportunity to be relieved of

the money operations, we find many reasons to hold on to this part, or that part, and in some cases to all of the decision-making that authorizes the money payment. Why?

Let us look at some observations we have made as we have experimented, and as we have seen others experiment with or attempt to implement the use of technical staff in eligibility and grant functions. Perhaps we can learn something about ourselves and our convictions.

Our first involvement with the separation of eligibility-grant functions from social services was early in 1965 when eligibility workers began to assist at intake and when California proposed a four-county experiment in the Old Age Security program. This Old Age Security project, with official federal waivers, operated from October, 1965, through September, 1967. The Marin County Board of Supervisors sanctioned our participation in this project and at the same time supported our efforts to develop a similar project which would apply to all programs. Almost overnight the Old Age Security demonstration, which permitted the use of a self-declaration and separated eligibility-grant functions from social service functions, changed the program from the one that was least attractive to many members of the social work staff to the prestige program in the department. It also produced ideas and staff pressure to operate in a similar fashion in the other programs.

Expansion of the project concept to all programs occurred during 1966, with final county acceptance and submission of the project proposal to the state agency early in November, 1966. Final waivers approving the department-wide demonstration project were received in late September, 1967, after almost eleven months of delay. During the spring of 1967 there were major shifts in federal policy in the direction of some of the project objectives, which spurred the final action allowing the experiment to take place.

We mention the time lag not to criticize those who had to make the decisions, but to indicate the extensive soul searching and the conflicts that existed at various hierarchical levels of policy-making. While we cannot blame all of the lag on the reaction to the proposal, a great deal of time appeared to be directed not toward frontal challenges of its objectives, as might be expected, but toward rather lengthy interactions with its ideas, vaguely stated reservations, and seeming postponement of positive action. Old traditions, rationalizations, and theories, unlike old soldiers, do not fade away; even without change of accepted objectives, experimentation with alternative means of achieving the objectives must run a difficult obstacle course. Conceptualization of needed change is the policy-maker's role. This did not come easily, and, we suspect, even now there is not real consensus, even majority consensus, about the wisdom of the changes taking place. Experimental projects, however, may permit us to gather material for decision-making based on some objective findings rather than on habit, untested theory, or assumptions about public welfare recipients. Why is it so hard to gain official support for experimentation?

Lag is not the only problem. The "band-wagon" approach, or what may be called the "administrative-directive-today-and-in-operation-tomorrow" approach, is as disturbing as the traditional preservationist approach. It is rather appalling to hear official visitors state that their administrator has decided to embark on the separation of eligibility and social services, and they are here to find out how to do it in time to implement the change next week or next month. This has hap-

pened several times. Some of the people assigned to develop
the planned changes were so against the principles involved
that it was difficult to see how the plan could be developed
incorporating the concepts. An administrative fiat and a set
of operating procedures alone will not produce results. It is
difficult to say "slow down" when the change is so long overdue, but a directive does not automatically achieve the intended objectives. The concepts involved in the change
challenge three decades of traditional practices founded
largely on rationalization, mystique about relationship and
method within a money-payment program, to say nothing of
the nightmarish complex of regulations, reports, and forms
to be dealt with to accomplish the ends. No one should expect instant adaptation of the existing system to the drastic
surgery required. We must be prepared for presurgical anx-
iety and postsurgical shock. No one should overlook the importance of staff development in attaining this adaptation,
in walking the long road from commitment to accomplishment, if not in comfort, at least with fewer shock fatalities.
The more appropriate term would be "staff redevelop-
ment."

Change—drastic change at a quick pace—necessitates not
only intensive learning but also intensive unlearning. It is
inevitable that all learning and unlearning be painful, but
it is evitable that it be depressing. As an integral and vital
part of administration it is the role of staff development to
help translate into practice the concept enunciated so poign-
antly by Charlotte Towle: "As the staff are done unto so
can they do unto the clients." [1] It is the role of staff development to help bridge the gap between word and deed, be-

[1] Charlotte Towle, *The Learner in Education for the Professions*
(Chicago: University of Chicago Press, 1954).

tween agency expectation and staff performance. I hasten to add that staff development in this context is a far cry indeed from the old, conventional, in-service training. It is the creative planning and execution of programs with truly relevant content and the learning and unlearning of experiences that make for true staff participation and involvement, the type of experience that provides for "thinking in a marrow-bone." [2]

Administration and line staff share many of the obstacles encountered between conceptualization and implementation. Let us look at some of the bone-marrow issues that arise; not at the idea, but at where one would draw the line in carrying out the idea in practice. There are questions to ask and to answer.

Can technical personnel determine eligibility and the amount of grant? If your answer is "yes," how far are you willing to go in practice?

1. Can they relieve the social workers by filling out the forms and clarifying information?

The answer is: "Yes, of course. Let us get rid of the paper work and do social work."

2. Can the technician review facts and apply them to criteria established for money payments?

"Well, probably," many will say.

3. Can technical staff interview recipients in order to ascertain the facts that are necessary to establish eligibility and the grant, and make the necessary independent decision?

Many will reply with a startled question: "You mean

2 "God guard me from those thoughts men think
In the mind alone;
He that sings a lasting song
Thinks in a marrow-bone."
(William Butler Yeats, "A Prayer for Old Age")

without social work supervision?" The answer to this question is not yet settled. Even at the policy-making level where the use of technical staff is supported, in the midst of talk about a guaranteed income, there is still a conviction that there should be social work supervision of eligibility and grant operations within the welfare structure. Witness the fact that not until April 1, 1969, was there an approved merit system classification in California for eligibility supervisors although the state now operates Old Age Security and Medical Assistance on a self-administered declaration form processed by eligibility technicians. For as long as we cannot relinquish the decision-making authority, we are not committed to a basic income plan or even to the separation of money payment and social services.

5. Do we believe that only a person classified as a social worker can treat others with respect and sensitivity, can interview and evaluate facts?

Our experience shows otherwise. We have to ask if we as social workers are better prepared to accept a delegation of activities than relinquishment of ultimate authority to make eligibility and grant decisions regarding money.

6. The key question thus arises: are we prepared for a truly separate money-payment system, or are we giving lip service to an idea?

Everyone who favors an income-maintenance plan will have to face this issue. It is a great idea—but where do we stand when it is *our* service case, and someone else makes the money decision without *our* review, direction, and authorization? In practice, many social workers are finding it difficult to release control over grant decisions which they regarded as "case decisions."

Many people have expressed concern about the separation

because it "confuses" the client, requires the applicant or recipient to "relate" to more than one person within the department, may require repetition of some data, or requires giving some types of information which the applicant may find difficult to talk about to technical staff. Many mourn the loss of the application interview as a means of engaging the applicant in service activities.

No one can deny that immediately after the change in operation there was some confusion as to whom a client should talk to, about what, and when. Concern is usually expressed in terms of client confusion, although close observation would indicate confusion shared between staff and client. The public welfare system is cumbersome, complex, and confusing at best, no matter what the staffing pattern. The additional confusion caused by separation of money and social service functions is quite noticeable in those who have had experience with the old system, whether the person is staff member or recipient. New staff and new applicants do not appear to have the same difficulty. We should guard, too, against quick assumptions about clients' reactions and determine whose reactions they really are, the client's or the worker's.

The other anticipated problems are more difficult to assess. Consistency of relationship, emotion-laden interview content, engaging the client in services—all are in-group concepts which elicit an immediate total response but not much examination of the context in which the terms are used. Let us look at relationship consistency in the public welfare setting as it is today. Is it a reality or a myth?

The organization of most welfare departments defies consistency of relationships. Some of the people who are most concerned about relationship consistency and service fragmentation raise no question about a department organization that requires a case to be transferred from section to section not on the basis of service needs, but because the grant program changes, a child moves from a foster home to his own home, or because of any other technicality. When section-to-section transfers are combined with transfers caused by staff turnover, reassignments, or promotions, it is very difficult to consider relationship consistency in the traditional public welfare department a reality factor. Another operational split will not solve this problem, of course, if we continue to organize services by traditional income categories instead of by service dimensions.

We should also look at our tendency to exploit the concept of relationship as the magic answer to all problems and at the implicit assumption that we have copyrighted its use by virtue of social work methodology. When relating is the problem, relationships may be critical. For a critical look at relationship in the public welfare setting, we might ask whether it is easier to relate to one person with two, sometimes inconsistent, roles, or to two people with different roles. Perhaps we should ask what happens when problem-focused services are interrupted for an eligibility review, an investigation of eligibility facts, or the updating of a social study which requires detailed information unrelated to the pressing immediate problem. In a few years the question of whether money and social services should be combined or separated will be academic, but for the present we must deal with the problem and its implications or be ill prepared for the separation.

Anticipation of problems when clients are asked to repeat data bears careful consideration in setting up the operational procedures of separated functional units and in training technical staff. However, because we are focusing on social work implications in the delivery of social services, some observations about a possible relationship between the repetition of data, difficulty in giving information, and the engagement of the applicant in service activities seem in order.

Perhaps there is data repetition because in the interview the social worker still uses an old technique that has become unfunctional. Perhaps some difficulty experienced by clients in sharing personal facts is due to the elaboration called for in a service interview and will be minimized in an eligibility interview or on a self-declaration form. Perhaps problems observed in giving emergency services to applicants are in part staff problems due to changing modes of approach. The possibility exists and should be given some consideration.

There is no doubt that social service workers have, in the course of years, developed interviewing techniques geared to obtaining factual data to establish eligibility. Making a virtue out of a necessity, the aid application has evolved into a service interview tool. The removal of the forms with their convenient entree demands a major revision in techniques for many who have become skilled in the public welfare interview method. The transition is difficult, and some social work staff will not make it. Yet, the eligibility interview route to social services, and the social worker who does not adapt to changing conditions, will soon be obsolete. The prospect is threatening to many, and some provision must be made to deal with this threat through training and experience with other techniques or, in some cases, by means of a change of classification and function for those who do not make the transition.

Let us return to those who are struggling to effectuate today's stated convictions. Do we believe that the right to receive money payments, based on established facts and criteria, can stand alone, separated from social work services? Many will say, "Yes, of course. Let us have the guaranteed income now." But let us look more closely at the facts. Picture yourself in a public welfare department. The applicant fills out a form to establish his eligibility for assistance. The form is processed by an eligibility technician. The social worker does not do an intake study upon application. Such a study must be activated at the request of the client, of an interested community person, or of the concerned eligibility technician who knows that referral is indicated if certain key questions are answered in a certain way. This is not a fantasy. It is the way our department is operating now under test conditions. The observations that follow are not based on the reactions of our staff alone, but also on those of our colleagues, of visitors, and those heard in discussions all over the country.

What about the elderly gentleman who applies for Old Age Assistance to supplement Social Security for himself and his wife? Many will say, of course, that this is no problem since the need for money is obvious. Others, some of those most knowledgeable about elderly recipients, will say that these elderly people may need medical attention, they may be isolated, or unable to care for themselves—we must find out and give whatever services are indicated. We cannot deny those observations. But let me ask another question. Do we know the relative incidence of these problems in the public assistance recipients as compared with Social Security or company pension recipients? That is a leading question, and the answer is not known. Why are we so much more concerned with, or committed to, the public assistance recipient? When they answer that question, some social workers will find that they have an inherent bias toward welfare applicants.

We become even more hesitant about letting go of the intensive intake study in which we identify need and then feel committed to give services to every AFDC recipient. What about the widow, the deserted family, the unmarried mother? Reactions to these problems in the abstract form a continuum. With the widowed family there is a little hesitancy; with a deserted family there are more reservations; and the unmarried mother has a hard time getting money without services. The selective factor in these situations allegedly is not the source of the family's income or its status designation, but the degree of difficulty that the family is experiencing. These situations along with some others instantly set off flashing red lights. The bold print in the service manual is clear, and the course we should take well defined. Sometimes we forget to look to the recipient, who may be a bit mystified by the amount of attention he is receiving, especially if the crisis was a few years back.

A captive recipient must be strong, assertive, and perhaps even aggressive to refuse services outright—especially when the helpful person appears to be so sure that there is something to talk about. This situation may seem exaggerated to the social worker and his agency, but do not discard the possibility too quickly. Having once discovered a problem that is causing or contributing to a difficulty, can we offer services and then permit the person in apparent distress to decide to work out the problem as he sees fit without accepting our offer? We sincerely believe in the recipient's right to use social services or not, but how free is the public welfare recipient to exercise this right?

It is time to look at our approaches to public welfare recipients. Are we acting in accordance with what we say we believe? Our inconsistencies are most noticeable in the AFDC program. For some reason we immediately take a paternal-protective attitude toward the AFDC applicant even though the children in the case already have one or two parents on the scene.

The social study is a perfect example of our insecurity about the family's functioning or, perhaps, about our own role with the family. By what moral or legal right do we intrude into every facet of family functioning because a family requires financial assistance? There may be a need or we want to provide help, some will say. Is this the way that we offer services to others, or do we put the recipient into a special category? How many family service workers go around knocking on neighborhood doors to study the health, social, psychological, and financial problems of each family member, to establish a service plan? Yet, in the name of services, many public welfare workers do just that. It is true that a recipient can refuse most services, but is he not suspect if we have discovered a problem, even a potential problem? We probably note on his record that he is "resistant." In some cases, if the client's "no" is not strong enough, the worker continues to maintain periodic contact "to establish a relationship," or "to support," or to be available when the recipient "sees the light" or gets into trouble. The recipient, in turn, learns the rules of the game on which his role as client is based.

What about our services? Those who do accept "services," actively or passively, receive those services in caseloads of sixty; that is, they receive regular "service" contacts when there are not too many other crisis families with priority demands on the worker's time, and if the worker is not busy on a crash program catching up with mandatory eligibility investigations, and if the department can recruit enough skilled workers to go around.

Is it not time to concentrate on those services we are capable of giving in relation to problems discovered by the recipients rather than on the search for problems? Perhaps if we try to do less, we can do more. Let us listen to those whom we seek to assist and not follow traditional routines.

Financial dependence is neither a social service hunting license nor the key to effective service. The situation may be, and probably is, a crisis. But let us face the fact that some recipients have more experience with, and resources to meet, a crisis than we have. Not all recipients require social work services at all times while on public assistance. Yet all recipients are assigned to a social worker with a "small" (usually 60 cases), or large (150 to 300 cases) caseload. We must ask ourselves why. What is our objective?

This brings us to another controversial idea under discussion and testing: the "banking" of cases in which the recipients do not need or cannot use services, or for whom we have no service resources. "Banking" in our department means eligibility and grant control status. Would you believe that in any given period of time more than a quarter of AFDC families, half of the ATD recipients, and about three quarters of the OAS recipients can do without a social worker in their lives? Further, there is great mobility in and out of service status. Our experience leads us to believe that "banking" is possible, even desirable. We are trying to learn more about this group of people; perhaps next year we can say more. Banking takes some effort and involves defining our services for the consumer. It takes an act of faith on the part of the state and on the part of the community to rely on the recipient to activate needed services or to permit him to live with his problem if he chooses. It also takes some humility along with good judgment to realize our limitations. Protective services and employment requirements are not valid reasons for many of our current practices.

It is time to bring our words and practices into concert or give up lip service to some of our concepts. Either we have something to offer as a service profession or we do not. Let us listen to the consumer, test our convictions, and find out.

ON FINDING
THE OLDER POOR

GENEVIEVE BLATT

PROJECT FIND, WHICH WAS LAUNCHED IN
the late spring of 1967 and completed in 1968, has been
based upon the belief that we have much yet to find out
about our fellow Americans who bear the double burden of
old age and poverty. The National Council on the Aging,
(NCOA), which developed the project, and the Office of
Economic Opportunity (OEO), which provided the funds
for NCOA to carry out the project in cooperation with the
OEO's community action agencies, were agreed that *they*
did not know enough. And they surmised that no one really
knew enough. So they started Project FIND to find out.

They wanted to determine with reasonable accuracy, how
many older people were poor, and how many of the poor
were old, and exactly where these older poor were. National
income, age, and social security statistics had already indicated the probable proportions of the problem, but it was
clear that there were wide local variations and that some, if
not many, of the older poor were so "invisible" that even

census takers had probably failed to count them. And as for knowing exactly where they were and who they were, even on a sample basis from which reasonable projections could be made, available information was much too scarce.

Besides locating and identifying the older poor, Project FIND was designed to discover their unmet needs, particularly to determine who and how many of them were *F*riendless, *I*solated, *N*eedy, or *D*isabled, adjectives which both describe too many of the older poor and conveniently provided the acronym which became the name of the project. Authorities in the field have been saying for years that too many older people suffer from a loneliness, a forced withdrawal from life, which is both a cruel punishment for them and a wasteful loss for the community. Gerontologists have been saying that too many of the aging are needlessly, or at least too soon, disabled and that they too often suffer from disabilities which could be relieved. Economists have been pointing out the economic problems caused when people live longer and longer on incomes which, at best, are seldom half as much as their preretirement incomes. But no one has known with any degree of precision how many older people in America endured one or more or all of these handicaps of old age, or who suffered from which of these or from some other such condition which a compassionate community could alleviate.

Finally, Project FIND was intended to demonstrate how the unmet needs of the older poor, once identified, could be met. This was to be done by referrals to existing services and by the establishment, in so far as funds would permit, of new services where required. Because of its experience with younger poor people, the OEO suspected that many of the older poor were unknown to social welfare agencies

which might have helped them. The ignorance, the alienation, the "invisibility" of so many of the poor were, the OEO
thought, probably characteristic to an even greater degree of
the elderly poor, who tend to be less educated, less mobile,
less "visible" than the younger poor or than the poor in
general. If younger people failed to use employment services
or other kinds of public aid because they did not know such
existed, or did not know how or where to apply, or were
afraid to apply, how much more likely that older people
would be eligible for help which they were not receiving,
and to which they could easily be referred. Furthermore, if
no help should be available for certain problems, how much
better it would be to know where the deficiency is and to
design a service to fill it than to run the risk of providing a
service which might either duplicate an existing one or
prove unnecessary because no one really needed it.

It must be remembered, of course, that Project FIND was
a demonstration project. It was never intended to apply on
a nationwide basis to even a sizable segment of the older
poor of America. Indeed, funds were so limited that the
most careful budgeting could extend it to twelve [1] areas
only, carefully chosen with special emphasis on insuring a
diversity of geographic locations, population density, type of
community, and so on. It was hoped that the twelve areas
would be representative enough and typical enough that
reasonable projections could be made from the findings, and
this proved to be the case.

It is to be hoped, of course, that the experience with Proj-

[1] Lower West Side, New York City; Phillipsburg, N.J.; Warren-Forest
counties, Pa.; Washington, D.C.; Huntington W. Va.; St. Petersburg,
Fla.; Alexandria, La.; Muskogee, Okla.; Lake County, Ind.; Pontiac,
Mich.; Santa Cruz County, Calif.; and Milan, Mo.

ect FIND will lead officials at all levels of government, as well as civic leaders, church groups, fraternal societies, and people in general, to bring about its extension into every area of the country. As a matter of fact, some such extension has already occurred, and a number of OEO community action agencies are already engaged in their own versions of Project FIND. We are encouraging others to follow suit as funds permit. Project FIND was merely a demonstration that "it *can* be done."

One other thing to be remembered about the contract for Project FIND, which the OEO negotiated with the NCOA, is that it was not limited to conducting the twelve demonstrations but included some other extremely important services and activities. Chief among these was the provision of competent technical assistance to OEO community action agencies interested in designing programs to meet the needs of their older poor. Expertise in the field of aging is scarce in this country. Some have said that people who really know what to do for the elderly and how to do it successfully are as hard to find now as child welfare experts were twenty or thirty years ago. Many community action agencies, recognizing the needs of the older poor, have had no idea how best to meet these needs and, amid the pressures of having to do something quickly for the poor in general, they have naturally tended to do most about what they knew most—meet the needs of children and young people. While there is a pronounced youth orientation in society in general and in the antipoverty programs in particular, not all the emphasis on youth is due to prejudice against old age. Much of it is due to not knowing *what* can be done or not even being sure that anything *can* be done. The field representatives whom the NCOA recruited, trained, and placed at the dis-

posal of the OEO community action agencies are doing a
job of education and assistance that is already bearing fruit.
It is showing up in many and varied programs throughout
the country in senior centers, food service programs, employment development and referral plans, home-help and
home-repair projects, transportation services, and so forth.
It will have much more effect as time goes on, particularly if
more funds become available.

The professionals supplied under its contract by the
NCOA have also been required to work with other OEO
agencies and to help in training state and local organizations and individuals who are enlisted to work with any
OEO programs. They have, for example, suggested how
VISTA (Volunteers in Service to America, sometimes called
the domestic Peace Corps) could use more older volunteers
and serve more older people. VISTA, already deeply aware
of the need in this field, has responded magnificently. In the
OEO Job Corps, intended to give young people a second—
perhaps a last—chance to develop employable skills, they
have suggested ways of recruiting and employing more older
people as instructors and counselors and of letting the train-
ees use their time and skills to aid the older poor in nearby
communities. They have pointed out the advantages of
using older aides in Head Start programs and older men
and women as helpers in neighborhood health and legal
centers. They have also reminded the health and legal service programs of some of the special needs of the older poor
which might otherwise have been overlooked. Indeed, when
the whole story of Project FIND is told, it may be found
that its greatest service was that of reminding those responsible for general types of community aid that the needs of the
older poor are a little different, in making clear just what

those needs are, and in suggesting how these general plans can easily be designed or redesigned to help the older poor without in any way detracting from the aid they provide for the younger people. Thus it may be that the older poor will come to be considered as an integral part of the community, rather than as an unfortunate group to be set apart, treated like lepers or even forgotten altogether.

The twelve demonstration areas covered by Project FIND have now completed their surveys and launched their own individual programs in answer to the major community needs of the older poor which they have discovered. Now that the series of training and orientation conferences and the hundreds of individual community consultations have been completed under the terms of the Project FIND contract, a report will be published. The report will not only provide some reliable data as to the location, identity, and needs of the older poor but also will offer many practical suggestions, with supporting statistical and anecdotal information, as to how these needs can effectively be met in any community where the will exists to meet them. It should be a landmark in the field.

But *there* may be "the rub."

Does a given community *have* the will to meet the needs of its older poor? Does the United States? Does a given state or locality? Do the people?

These are questions for which Project FIND can *not* provide the answers.

These answers are locked in the hearts of 200 million Americans, most of whom are enjoying longer lives, better health, and more affluence than any people anywhere at any time have ever enjoyed.

These answers are locked in the hearts of the elected representatives of the American people, the Congressmen, the state legislators, the local councilmen and commissioners, who determine governmental policies and levy the taxes to pay for them.

These answers are locked in the hearts of the elected and appointed leaders of the American people, the President and federal agency heads, the governors and their administrative aides, and all the thousands of mayors and supervisors and others who handle local government affairs.

These answers are locked in the hearts of the civic and community leaders across America, that army of "movers and shakers" who devote their spare time to public affairs and to whom the governmental leaders look for ideas and support.

And certainly, these answers are locked in the hearts of our older people themselves, who, if they should ever decide to complain, to show their strength at the ballot box and in neighborhood councils, could demand and *get* a change quickly.

If social workers were to decide, each in his own heart, and all together out of their collective knowledge and experience, that the double burden of old age and poverty should be and could be lifted from the shoulders of their fellow Americans, there would be an easing of that burden in a matter of days. In fewer years than anyone would guess, it could be lifted altogether.

If the social workers in every part of this nation could make their fellow Americans realize that at least 30 percent of the old in America are poor, and that at least 20 percent of the poor of America are old, something would be done.

If social workers were to say loudly and clearly that the median income of the American who is sixty-five years of age or older is less than half the median income of the American who is sixty-four years of age or younger, something would be done.

If social workers were to proclaim that a country which dishonors its old by leaving so many millions of them friendless, isolated, needy, and disabled is also defrauding its young by depriving them, not only of the contributions to society which the old can still make, but of their own hope to grow old in decency and dignity and independence, something would be done.

Project FIND has shown what needs to be done and suggested what can be done.

Social workers can help decide what *will* be done!

THE NEW UNIONISM IN
THE PROFESSION

MITCHELL I. GINSBERG
AND BERNARD M. SHIFFMAN

WE ARE NEITHER LABOR MANAGEMENT NOR
public administration experts. We are battle-weary, battle-
tested social workers who have worked on both sides of the
labor-management table, from the social service employees'
strike in the private sector in the 1950s to the social service
employees' strike in the public sector in 1967. During these
years we accumulated some experience and made our observations, drew some conclusions, and we admit to some
biases. One of our observations is that there are differences
in degree and perhaps in feeling, but the basic issues in the
current unionism of professionals are similar to those in the
earlier years.

After the Second World War, labor organized the white-
collar and professional workers, in and out of public service.
These new unions won major strikes for improvement in
wages, conditions of work, and other contractual terms.
Warmed by the passing of the Wagner Act, and by a sympa-

thetic National Labor Relations Board, union organization
and collective bargaining, stimulated by economic prosperity, became the American way of life. Industrial unions
made progress, moving from 4 million members in 1936 to
18 million in 1945. Unionism spilled over into the social
services "industry," which was desperately engaged with twin
problems. On the one hand, it was struggling to establish itself as a profession with all that goes with it; on the other
hand, it was trying to lift itself from a "female-dominated,
do-good-for-pin-money" type of employment to a field which
could support male heads of households. The ambitious,
college-oriented children of immigrants found social service
a vehicle for upward mobility and for status. To this comparatively new field they brought their parents' interest in
unionism. In the workingman's home the union was a way
of life, a religion; it was the "New Left."

Unionism was in the 1930s the peace movement and the
"folk-song cradle" locked into one. Craft and industrial
unionism was brought into the field of social welfare *in
toto,* including "the right to strike." A union without its
weapon was not a union. Even the ladylike YWCA caught
the fever and had a militant union in the period following
the Second World War. However, questions as to the use of
the strike, involvement of members and clients in union actions, need for emergency coverage, and the special problems created by work stoppage in institutions, hospitals, and
so on, were widely and inconclusively debated.

A mixture of "red-baiting," McCarthy style, interunion ri-
valry, organized unions' fear of liberal union members, and
boards of directors' fear of militant, aggressive unions, plus
the ill-timed use of the strike, reduced the union movement
in social work to memories so indistinct that current union

leaders are unaware they were using the same name as the earliest social work union—the Social Service Employees Union (SSEU). The issue in the 1950s was comparatively simple; it was clearly that of the right of employees to organize, to select their own bargaining agents.

In the last decade the conflict about the role of unions in social work has been more concentrated and more bitter in the public sector than in the voluntary. Here, it has become part of the over-all struggle about the place of unions in government, especially in municipal government. Certainly, this has been one of the areas in which most of the rapid growth in unionism has taken place. In New York City specifically, the toughest, costliest, and most bitter labor disputes have been between the city and some municipal unions. Despite the development of new labor-management machinery on both the city and the state level, it would be very optimistic and perhaps even foolhardy to predict that serious disputes do not still lie ahead. We have speculated, perhaps from a somewhat biased point of view, that many municipal unions are in a mood and a stage of development not unlike that of the industrial unions in the 1930s. If this is so, we can probably only look forward to continued difficulties until perhaps a more mature stage of development is reached by both sides. Certainly such issues as the relationship of unions to the Civil Service, to supervising and other employee associations, to client groups and welfare rights organizations, and so on, pose special problems for labor-management relations in the public welfare field.

It is this new role of unions in the public sector that we wish to explore. To some administrators even the concept of a union challenges their idea of public management. Some public authorities question whether government can retain the authority to govern effectively and protect the public interest under a regime of collective bargaining, even if the last step is only compulsory arbitration and not a strike action.

While in the private sector it is generally recognized that a union may strike and the employer may lock them out, in the public sector even some of the union members question use of the ultimate weapon—the strike. Some even question whether public servants *have* the unionist weapon, the *right* to strike. There is more universal agreement that "the right of the employees is that of participating effectively in the determination of their conditions of employment, and not the right to strike." [1]

From our review of the current labor-management literature and from our own experience we concur that there are no absolutes in this area. The right to organize, to be represented by a legal organization of the employees' own choosing, is no longer questioned. The public, however, will decide finally how far it will permit public servants to go—and that decision may vary in regard to public social welfare, education, sanitation, police, and firemen and be viewed differently depending on time, political climate, and so forth. Our position is that a viable union-administration system is essential in today's society.

On the other hand, can a union really be effective if it is denied the use of the so-called "ultimate weapon"? If one thinks of compulsory arbitration as the answer, other problems quickly turn up. Labor unions have traditionally opposed the idea of having someone, even an impartial arbitrator, make decisions that are binding. There are real po-

1 Kenneth O. Warner, ed., *Collective Bargaining in the Public Service* (Chicago: Public Personnel Association, 1967).

litical and legal questions involved in whether a city or any public agency or government unit can give this power and authority to anybody else. The government unit will also point out that it often does not have the money to meet union demands, and that it does not sell a product whose price can be increased to meet increased costs. The unions will respond that their members should not be expected to subsidize the city, and both sides are probably right.

In the New York *Times*, April 11, 1968, Mr. Joseph Loftus reported from Washington that a Presidential review committee established to study labor-management relations in the federal government would recommend binding arbitration as an alternative to the right to strike. The committee would further recommend establishment of a three-member board with authority to hand down binding rulings when impasses develop in negotiations of a basic labor agreement in the federal service. A grievance that remained unresolved after mediation would be referred to a third person. His decision would be binding in principle, if not in law. A more significant committee recommendation was for exclusive recognition where a majority of employees in a unit choose the union. The scope of issues which can be bargained still remains unresolved with all unions and especially with federal employees who now number about one million, adding 250,000 members since 1962.

The dilemma is: How do employees, teachers, social workers, or police gain effective participation in the determination of their conditions of employment without the right to strike? How do we define the legitimate scope of bargaining? One complication is that the public sector is regulated by the Civil Service Commission, usually at a level far removed from the bargaining unit. The civil service establishes rules governing the use of competitive examinations which control hiring and promotions, rules governing wage increases, grievance procedures, retirement benefits, health insurance, vacations, sick leave, and other terms of employment.

Civil service legislation is to the public sector the counterpart of collective bargaining in the private sector. Conditions of employment in the public sector, by this civil service legislation, become a legal right of the employee.

Another complication is that many government officials do not see how their authority can be shared with employees, given the Constitution, laws, and regulations.

A third complication is that in some states laws have been enacted to ban strikes in the public sector. The penalties proposed have been impractical and do little more than expose the impotence of the state government. As a matter of fact, the rash of strikes of public employees has made government-employee relations a part of the crisis of maintaining law and order in our cities.

A fourth complication, true in both the public and the private sector, is that

Too many companies, moreover, purchased peaceful relations at the expense of efficiency, granting concessions in the negotiation and administration of contracts which severely hampered the exercise of management initiative. . .

Inexperienced management . . . confronted by powerful unions . . . found it easier to practice appeasement than to accept the sterner task of organizational reform required by the advent of unionism. Appeasement naturally stimulated excessive demands . . . such as wildcat strikes and coercive tactics . . . slow-downs.[2]

2 Robert M. Macdonald, "Collective Bargaining in the Postwar Period," *Industrial and Labor Relations Review*, XX (1967), 555.

Also, at least from the point of view of administrators, inappropriate concessions were often made to keep down the dollar cost of the settlement. Substituting such concessions for a reasonable wage package simply meant that both groups ended up frustrated and unhappy, and peace and good will were entirely absent.

The absence of good will, the fear of change, and mutual suspicion—all barriers to successful collective bargaining—are the natural products of immaturity in labor-management relations in the public sector. This current condition arose from two factors in particular. First, in many instances public administrators have been insensitive to, and have failed to adjust voluntarily to, current changes, including the crumbling of the divine rights of sovereigns and public authorities. Second, poor staff relations, compounded by poor or "poverty-type" administration, have provided the new social work unions with strong issues around which they could organize and maintain union discipline. On the other hand, the insensitivity of public unions to matters of public interest—failure to relate salary demands to service in qualitative or quantitative terms—and their inability to adjust to the legitimate demands of a changing technology and provide for the entry of less skilled manpower into the social services have strengthened the public agencies' ability to resist even the legitimate union demands to participate in decisions which affect them. These two factors have stimulated use of the strike in the public sector, and a profusion of public employees' strikes in social welfare, police, sanitation, hospitals, and education has resulted. It has become obvious that neither the new unions nor the old public administrators can tolerate the maintenance of this collision course. Both the unions and the administrators need to develop a substitute for the strike technique—to create a more useful procedure for the resolution of conflicts, for providing government employees with a more effective voice in the determination of their terms of employment, and a means of keeping pace with wage scales in the private sector.

Are alternatives to strikes available to social welfare unions in the public sector? Compulsory arbitration has been proposed from time to time as the alternative to strikes. It is of more than passing interest that both unions and employers are unalterably opposed to compulsory arbitration for different reasons.

Great Britain, Australia, and New Zealand have successfully adopted compulsory arbitration. According to Jacob Finkelman, in considering arbitration one must weigh the advantages or disadvantages of a negotiated settlement. In Ontario, collective bargaining has survived in spite of the availability of arbitration. Mediation (intervention for the purpose of reconciling the two parties to help them break down the issues into manageable pieces) is another instrument. Fact-finding, with or without the authority to make recommendations, is another technique utilized in collective bargaining. All of these are tools which can only be useful when there is a clear definition of the scope of bargainable issues and set guidelines for arbitration. Since neither compulsory arbitration nor strikes seem appropriate in union-management relationships in the public or private sector, somebody must develop workable alternatives.

Issues such as emergency coverage of certain types of programs remain a problem. What happens to a children's institution that provides care on a twenty-four-hour live-in basis when most of the staff walks out? It has to be understood by everybody that no government unit or community will permit such a service to go unstaffed. Unless appropriate coverage can be worked out between management and the unions, other ways will be found to deal with the situation. In one of our two recent strikes (or "work stoppages," as they are somewhat euphemistically called), the bulk of the staff remained on the job, and no emergency developed. In the other case, a substantial number of volunteers offered their services, and between the volunteers, the supervisory staff, and a number of others who continued working, no really serious problem developed. It seems to us essential that in any "strike" a system for differentiating among various services ought to be worked out in advance. We do think that agreement about some pattern of emergency coverage of certain programs is essential for the children or patients involved and manifestly in the self-interest of the unions as well as of management.

Successful avoidance of strikes is possible only if we can perfect procedures and policies to provide effective alternatives to conflict. Grievance procedures must be readily available to deal with day-by-day disputes, and the employees should be represented by their elected unions. The recognition and certification of a public union should be an affirmation that it does *not* assert the right to strike. At the same time, employee organizations should have procedures available through which to initiate charges of unfair labor practices against the employing agency. Since civil service legislation is so vital, employee unions and administrators need to work together, negotiate, and submit jointly their requests for the legislative changes which will affect the terms of employment.

In our judgment, by far the most complicated and frustrating issue is the question of the scope of collective bar-gaining. We believe that this may well become even more troublesome and, in fact, may be the basic cause of most of the serious disputes that are likely to occur. Increasingly, some of the unions in the public sector feel that it is essen-tial to bargain collectively on a wide range of issues that management feels strongly lie within their prerogative. How to meet the legitimate aspirations of the unions while at the same time making it possible for management to carry out its appropriate responsibilities has simply not been resolved to anybody's satisfaction.

As worn-out veterans of two strikes and countless demon-strations, stoppages, "work-ins," we do not pretend to be fully objective. From our point of view, with which others will no doubt differ, the most important single cause of these troubles has been the union's attempt to bargain on items that were either illegal, beyond the department's abil-ity or competence to do anything about, or clearly within management's responsibility. A particular stumbling block in negotiations has been the union's efforts to involve clients in negotiations, picketing, and so on. Presumably, professional ethics would mean that neither side would in-volve clients or members in such disputes. Good will and good intentions by themselves are not enough to cover the organizational needs of the union officials. In our case, con-stant harassment and blocking of innovation have made a working relationship impossible. Perhaps the rules of the game are now to be changed, but the profession ought to think it through carefully, since change in rules can affect either team.

Certainly, there are very few people today who would question the need for drastic reform in the welfare system.

As outspoken advocates of such changes we have sought and welcomed support from all groups and individuals. We do not doubt the genuine interest of the unions in such reforms, although at times there is considerable ambivalence due to the conflict between union self-interest and community welfare. But we do not think that a labor-management contract is the vehicle for such changes. For example, we agree that welfare clients should be entitled to telephones. But to make a demand for telephones a part of collective bargaining, especially when it was well known that the city did not have the authority to grant them, seems to us to be at least confused and naïve if not cynical and dishonest.

On other issues that seem to us more appropriately subject to collective bargaining, some reasonable and balanced approach must be worked out. We would agree that the union has a stake in personnel transfer policies, even though for a long time these have reasonably been defined as management's responsibility. But an agreement to prevent indiscriminate transfers has been so misinterpreted by the union as to prevent transferring a worker from one unit to another without seeking volunteers for the job from all over the city. This has been true even when the transfer simply meant moving from one desk to another. Such inflexibility can only lead to chaos and disruption of service to clients.

As we have indicated, we know no perfect solution for this problem of defining the scope of negotiations. New York City has set up an Office of Collective Bargaining with representatives from the unions, the public, and the city. This office has taken a definitive position through the decisions of impartial mediators on what is and what is not bargainable. To us, this approach offered some hope of a fair and sound solution. Unfortunately for us, and we believe for all the people of New York City, one of the two key unions in the welfare field has refused to participate in the Office of Collective Bargaining.

The difficulty is compounded in dealing with a union that wants to be treated in a professional manner but often, ambivalently, behaves like an industrial union, resisting all changes equally, including those which might make for greater efficiency and those which might improve services to clients. When we attempted to undertake an experiment, for example, so that workers could in fact provide direct service to clients, the two major unions united and prevented us from initiating a federally funded demonstration program.

There are other problems that defy simple solutions. What can be done when there are several competing unions in the same department and each one feels the need to outdo the other? What about the fact that increasingly the union leadership does not seem able to speak for the membership? Agreements made in good faith are often overthrown by the membership, and union leaders will often say that "the situation is out of our hands."

Likewise, what about the problems that arise when administrators enter into agreements with a union, and then encounter such resistance among middle-management staff that the agreements are not carried out in good faith? Unions may well find negotiations frustrating because more than one level of government may have to be involved. In New York City, for example, the policies and regulations of the State Department of Social Services have much to do with what the local department can and cannot negotiate.

In our experience we have found that the new unionists in

the professions respect pure power more than pure reason. It is abundantly clear that sit-ins, teach-ins, and strikes hurt first the client, secondly the agency, and finally the staff as well. No one wins in a war. In a short five-year period, New York City's Department of Social Services had two major strikes and at least twenty demonstrations. Have the social service unions won great victories in this fashion? Winning the right to recognition was a great victory, but after that we think not!

Clearly, it is easier to outline the issues than to spell out the answers. As we have indicated, collective bargaining is almost certain to become more prevalent in the public social welfare field. In the more immediate future, disputes and work stoppages are likely to grow in number. As welfare departments move toward the inevitable reorganization of staff and the wide use of aides, these disputes will probably become more embittered. Cities and states are increasingly apt to pass legislation defining the rules of the game, but to what extent these will be effective is by no means certain. Moreover, the presence or absence of professional social workers in top administrative positions probably will not make much difference. We took office as liberal, pro-union administrators with what we at least believed were progressive attitudes toward labor relations. Today we are sadder and, we hope, wiser, though it would certainly be difficult to find any evidence of substantial improvement in this crucial area.

What we all must understand is that both unions and management are primarily in business to provide services to people, and in the end their interests have to get priority, or at least equal time. This means the acceptance of change by all of us and *that* never comes easily. Whether we like it or not, the scope of collective bargaining will inevitably expand. Whether it makes organizational sense or not, unions will succeed in winning their demands that additional items be covered by collective bargaining. On the whole, we think this can be constructive. At any rate, it is bound to happen. It is even more certain that the clients or consumers will have a steadily increasing role in policy formulation and implementation. For administrators and management generally, this may be hard to accept, but they will be wise to anticipate and respond to it. By the same token, unions will have to recognize that they will not get all they want. Public opinion is sensitive in many of these areas, and the dislike of disruptive activity in the public sector is deeply held. Also, the demands of clients and consumers introduce a new factor, and they may not always be consistent with what union members feel are in their organization's best interests. All of us are going to have to be more flexible, knowledgeable, and sophisticated, and if our experience is indicative, ready for round-the-clock negotiating sessions.

There are no absolutes except change, which demands a creative flexibility on both sides of the table. The door is open for such creative, reorganizing activity. If we learned anything from our days and nights of negotiating, it was the slogan of our labor advisor, "Don't kick an open door!"

P.L. 90-248 AND
HOMEMAKER SERVICES

EUNICE MINTON

THE HOMEMAKER-home-health aide service effectively serves both social and health needs; it is readily understandable and widely endorsed by users and supporters alike; and the time has come for it to expand tremendously. An added distinction is that it is hotly pursued by two professions, with social work and medicine each claiming homemaker services as its own by right of birth or adoption.

Such distinctive achievements have resulted from decades of dedicated work, from the days of the informal Committee on Homemaker Services to the current prestigious National Council for Homemaker Services, Inc. But homemaker service has demonstrated to a high degree the pervasive impact of another key element: the readiness to respond and the flexibility to adapt to varying human needs. Starting as a service to care for children whose mothers were hospitalized, it has steadily added other purposes, such as functioning as a member of a treatment team. In addition, homemaker service has pioneered in showing how to make the most effective use of available staff through assignments based upon differentiated needs. Other social and health programs have only recently given attention to this critical aspect of program planning.

The evolvement of any service is affected by developments in other programs or services. Medicare and Medicaid to meet health needs and the 1962 public welfare amendments to meet social needs have substantially affected in different ways the nature, purpose, and expansion of homemaker service. These and other developments during the past six years have brought about increased recognition of the necessity for a better balance between out-of-home and in-home care and services to meet social and health needs. The serious lack of in-home services has meant for too long that there were no alternatives to nursing homes for many of the aged or to foster care for some children. Greater recognition of, and resources to meet, the wide variations in individual needs, coping capacities, desires, and supportive resources is long overdue in our society. Homemaker service has firmly established itself as a major in-home service of great effectiveness and therefore should benefit enormously from further emphases on the expansion of in-home services.

The nature and timing of new, and changes in old, federal programs greatly affect developments under both voluntary and public auspices and sometimes result in a disbalance. For example, the federal legislation and funding for medical care and services under titles XVIII and XIX certainly assure medical care for more individuals than were covered in the past, but this emphasis by itself can result in a disbalance in the development of the health and social resources that are necessary to deal effectively even

with the health problems of many people. Homemaker service is experiencing this disbalance as it attempts to relate
to the definition of, and conditions for, home health aides
under these titles. However, sometimes subsequent federal
legislation authorizes other programs and funding that help
to overcome the disbalancing impact of previous programs.
As a case in point, I believe that the 1967 welfare amendments provide opportunities to achieve a better balance in
health and social services and to make possible a continuum
of service when such is needed.

These amendments will have considerable effect on the
AFDC and child welfare programs and to a minimum extent on the programs for the aged, the blind, and the disabled. They offer specific opportunities for the tremendous
expansion of homemaker service. If these amendments are
fully utilized, there is no question that homemaker service
would be established in almost all geographic areas, that
present programs would be significantly expanded, and
that homemaker service would meet a broader range of
needs in a greater variety of ways.

Four of the amendments with over-all implications are of
special interest. First, as of July 1, 1968, child welfare and
AFDC services must be combined into single organizational
units in all state and local welfare departments to carry out
a single program of services for families and children (not
applicable where there were separate agencies for these two
programs). This means that there are no longer any separate services, such as homemaker service, for child welfare
and AFDC cases. This combining of services should greatly
facilitate a total approach in public welfare planning, both
in developing and supervising its own homemaker programs
and in taking a leadership role in cooperative community

planning for homemaker service. It also may remove many of the problems experienced by other agencies that provide homemaker service, such as having to deal with two programs for families and for children, with different conditions and funding potentials. Nationally, under the new Social and Rehabilitation Service, AFDC and child welfare services have been integrated under the Children's Bureau.

Secondly, the authorization to give services to families beyond those who receive public assistance permits reaching more families, e.g., families who are current applicants for financial assistance; those who are receiving Medicaid only; those likely to become recipients of financial assistance within five years, including those in low-income neighborhoods or census tracts. For example, all families in a public housing project could be included, and so could all families using a homemaker program in a poverty neighborhood center or in a poverty census tract. This liberalization opens up the very real potential of reaching practically all low-income families.

The third amendment concerns federal funding. The rate of federal financing of the costs of all services, including homemaker service in AFDC, was raised to 85 percent for the period ending July 1, 1969, after which it returns to 75 percent. Few programs offer on a continuous basis as much as three dollars for every dollar of state and local money for any purpose. Thus there is a sizable amount of federal funding available for homemaker service. A related change, and one significant to homemaker service, is that the authorization to purchase services from other state public agencies was extended to include purchase from any source, under conditions established by the Secretary of Health, Education, and Welfare. The same rate of federal matching applies to the purchase of services. A similar amendment was also made to the programs for the aged, the blind, and the disabled.

We all welcome this long-needed flexibility that will enable public welfare departments to carry out their responsibilities under the AFDC program with the full cooperation and participation of other community resources. This change also facilitates community planning to determine the most suitable auspices for homemaker service, without the former limitations on sources of funding. Use of the purchase provision will require greater attention to methods of ascertaining the cost of homemaker service. For example, what items are to be included? Are there to be differences in costs related to the purpose and nature of the purchased homemaker service, and how will this be determined? The services that may be purchased must be provided by qualified agencies or individuals who are either licensed to provide such services or are otherwise approved. In respect to these aspects of purchase, the Social and Rehabilitation Service, the states, and homemaker service agencies will want the guidance and standards of the National Council for Homemaker Services.

The fourth amendment with over-all implications required public welfare departments, no later than July 1, 1969, to train and use subprofessional personnel in their service programs. Homemaker service should be immediately affected by this change because homemakers are within this classification of personnel; public welfare believes in and knows what is involved in securing and training homemakers; and public welfare is knowledgeable as to what tasks homemakers can effectively carry out. Public welfare, like all social and health agencies, knows that if nonprofessionals are to be appropriately and productively used in direct services, it is crucially important that there be clarity as to the purposes of such use; as to the particular service functions or tasks that can be effectively performed by persons with limited educational preparation; as to the personal qualities and experience required; and as to the training and supervision that are necessary to promote the growth and productivity of such personnel and for agency accountability. Another essential component is assurance of maximum opportunities for formal and technical education that will enable subprofessional personnel to move upward in the career system.

The reasons most often given for incorporating nonprofessionals in social and health programs are the current manpower shortage and the lack of jobs for the poor. In my judgment, these reasons are not in themselves sufficient grounds for sound inclusion of subprofessional personnel in our social and health systems. The only solid basis is that these people have contributions to make that are essential if there are to be comprehensive and constructive approaches to alleviating and preventing social and health problems. The fact that such inclusion broadens the total manpower potential and provides needed employment to persons of low income certainly adds very welcome and needed corollary benefits. Homemaker service should be alert both to the values and problems that may result from implementing this mandate.

And now we come to the amendments that set forth specific social objectives and authorize or require a broad range of services to achieve these objectives.

The basic service amendment to AFDC is an "umbrella" one in that the objectives of the other amendments fall within its over-all aims. This amendment requires every public welfare department to institute a program of family and child welfare services for parents and their children with the purpose of maintaining and strengthening family life, retaining or attaining capacity for self-support and care, and fostering child development. Family and child welfare services are defined in broad terms, and all such services are authorized for federal matching of funds. It is of special interest that family services are now defined in federal law for the first time. Some of the specific responsibilities under this broad provision indicate the range of needs to which homemaker services would be directed, such as, for example, protective service for children, improving home and child care and money management, and giving attention to the health of parents and children.

From its beginning, homemaker service has been both a family and a child welfare service and has long demonstrated that it is specific to the purpose of maintaining and strengthening family life and fostering child development. The indicated range of needs is familiar to, and has been served in a variety of ways by, most homemaker programs. The new implications are more a matter of emphasis and extension. For example, the singular contribution of homemaker services in protective services is well known, but they are not widely used for this purpose. I have always thought that homemaker service should be used in every case where children are, or are likely to be, endangered by inadequate parental care and protection. In doing so, the social agency would have the assurance that it had utilized all appropriate resources in trying to improve parental functioning. It would also aid in agency assessment of the potentials for parental change and of the consequences of decisions to refer or not to refer to the court for removal of the children.

The use of homemaker service for educational purposes

will have to be greatly extended if parents who cannot benefit from community educational resources are to have the
help they need to overcome the gaps in their knowledge of
the proper care of their homes and children, and of income
management. In view of current practices in some market
places, training in respect to money management must give
more emphasis to consumer education, including the personal and legal ways by which consumer interests and rights
can be protected.

The wide range and volume of health problems in AFDC
and other low-income families indicate a great demand for
the personal care function of homemaker service and for extensive educational efforts in good health practices. With
the greatly heightened interest in, and need for, education
in everyday living and functioning, and the demonstrated
success of agencies that use group approaches, the homemaker service field might well give further consideration to
its role in group education, including combinations of in-
home training and group approaches. I urge, too, that
homemaker service plan and consciously emphasize ways
whereby it can help parents in low-income groups to gain
confidence in the exercise of their citizenship roles and
rights.

Another amendment requires public welfare departments
to provide services that will help parents and youth to ac-
quire capability for employment and to attain self-sufficiency.
The departments must assist all adults and youth to obtain
the maximum amount of readiness for training and employment. Referrals are to be made to the Department of Labor,
which, under the legislation, is required to provide opportunities for training and employment to parents and youth
considered suitable by the welfare departments. Referral is

not made for youths age sixteen and over who are in school or shortly will reenter, or to persons who have to care for ill family members. The law also specifically stipulates that no parent or parent substitute may be referred unless adequate child care services are available for the periods of time the parent is in training or employment.

The Department of Labor is initiating its program, primarily in two hundred urban localities and is mandated to make every effort to reach all sections of the states with training and employment resources. It is anticipated that over a period of time, large numbers of adults and youth will be referred to the Department. Hence this joint welfare-labor endeavor will grow rapidly, and so will the need for child care services.

The need for child care services offers the most immediate and specific opportunity for homemaker service. The report of the House Ways and Means Committee [1] identifies day care and homemaker service as child care services. Therefore, child care services are interpreted broadly to include both in-home and out-of-home services, with homemaker service as a major in-home service. Homemaker service for this purpose must be so organized as to respond promptly and to provide service for the varying hours of the day and varying periods of time that may be required by the parent's or caretaker's training or employment.

Another predictable need is for in-home emergency service. Crises will occur when there is a breakdown in the regular plan for out-of-home care. Children who are regularly cared for in day care facilities may not be able to go to them for a day or two because of colds or other minor reasons.

[1] Social Security Amendments," Report of the Committee on Ways and Means on H.R. 12080, House Report No. 544, p. 98.

Emergencies will require service until the crisis is over. Short-term services will also be needed while other plans are being made for the care of some children.

Fulfillment of the requirement that child care services be "adequate" will be assured by: (1) all out-of-home services (family group homes and day care centers) being licensed, or approved as meeting the standards for licensure; and (2) all in-home services, including homemaker service, meeting standards established by the state welfare departments. In general, standards for homemaker services have not been developed to the point of objective use in evaluating individual programs. The National Council for Homemaker Services would be a major resource for materials that could be recommended to the states for such use. This offers a tremendous opportunity to promote solid programs and to upgrade some of the current ones.

There is another significant implication to the requirement for adequacy of services: the great need for day care facilities will have concentrated attention. There has been considerable joint planning for greatly expanded day care with the Office of Economic Opportunity (OEO) and other national groups. All day care funded through the Department of Health, Education, and Welfare or OEO must meet the requirements jointly promulgated by these agencies. These requirements include particular standards in respect to enrichment programs for the children. Enrichment opportunities for children who do not have them in their own homes and who have been isolated from those in the community should have the special attention of all services in and out of the home. I suggest that the homemaker service field consciously emphasize this objective and plan how homemaker programs can either provide or participate in

making greatly needed enrichment opportunities available
to the children they serve.

The anticipated increase in the demand for in-home child
care services offers rich opportunities, but it also presents
some issues that the homemaker service field will have to resolve for itself. How will the provision of ongoing and emergency child care services affect the purposes and capabilities
of homemaker service? Will homemakers be required to
have any different qualifications, skills, or training? Will
the expansion of homemaker service adversely affect
achievement of the other objectives of homemaker service?
Should homemaker service be used for this child care only
in combination with other homemaker functions, such as
parent education or education in personal care? Are there
ways of organizing the total service so that all the purposes
of homemaker service, including child care, may be protected?

These are the kinds of issues that face any service whose
time for significant expansion has come. Satisfactory answers
cannot be found without consideration of the consequences
of alternatives. For example, if it were decided that homemaker service should not provide emergency child care service, it is certain that some type of service, such as baby sit-
ters, would be organized to meet this need. The implications of such a development for homemaker service itself
and for its concern about in-home services would have to be
weighed. From my vantage point, which is limited to seeing
the great need for, and respecting the capabilities of, homemaker service, I can only urge that homemaker service respond to this new demand as it has to others in the past.
Certainly, much experimentation and demonstration are
essential if we are to plan and organize homemaker service

programs that can respond with equal effectiveness to such widely different needs.

The legislation also requires public welfare departments to carry out programs with the objective of preventing, as well as reducing the incidence of, births out of wedlock. This, too, presents opportunities for the extended use of homemaker service. It is obvious that neither homemaker service nor any other single service can achieve this goal. However, our knowledge and experience in respect to this problem encourage us to believe in the effectiveness of a comprehensive service and a coordinated community approach. Homemaker service must be a part of such a package. In implementing this provision, priority attention is to be given to current out-of-wedlock pregnancies, to mothers with children born out of wedlock within the past two years, and to youths living in conditions that are conducive to births out of wedlock. The kinds of problems associated with these characteristics and conditions immediately suggest the need for traditional homemaker service: prospective mothers are hospitalized for childbirth, and many will need homemaker service during this period; some families will need homemaker service because the mother is seriously overburdened with home and child care and perhaps part-time employment; some families will need homemaker service because of maternal mental or physical handicaps, and some because of neglect or abuse of the children.

I urge special attention for still another group. These are the unmarried teen-age mothers with their first child who are faced with so many changes in their lives and with new and hard decisions to make. Many are isolated from the normal support of family and friends and have little or no knowledge about caring for their babies or organizing their daily activities. Completion of high school by unmarried teen-age mothers is not permitted by some schools, or it may be permitted through special arrangements, such as allowing them to attend special night or day classes. We know that these girls must have comprehensive and coordinated services if they are to surmount the difficulties presented by their situation. Counseling, special school classes, group training in child care, and advice on family planning have been partially successful. But it seems to me that another ingredient should be added: homemaker service to provide practical application of what is learned in group discussions about child and home care. As a member of the team, the homemaker can contribute to the service objective through her assessment of the girls' capacities, interests, and limitations and through her opportunities to provide much needed encouragement for the efforts that these girls do make. Homemaker service is essential even for the one objective of assisting these girls to complete high school and prepare for employment. Research suggests that unmarried teen-age girls who finish high school are less likely to repeat pregnancies out of wedlock than are those who drop out of school. Surely we can use our social and health resources to help these girls complete high school and have vocational training.

Two additional services are included in the amendments. Family-planning services must be offered to all appropriate persons, and emergency assistance and services may be provided if the states so choose. Family planning is defined in federal policy to include social, medical, and educational services. Since this service is applicable both to the married and the unmarried, it is reasonable to assume that some of them will also need homemaker service. The authorization

of emergency assistance and services will fill a long and unhappy void. Money payments, medical care, and social services may be provided to those under the age of twenty-one
and to their parents to meet emergencies. Since this
authorization is not limited to AFDC families, more families and children may now be included for services. Because
homemaker service has long been used to help families at
times of emergency, this amendment too will undoubtedly call for an expansion of homemaker services.

All of these amendments will apply to over one and a
quarter million families with close to four million children
receiving public assistance. These families, with a multitude
of social and health problems, have an as yet untapped rich-
ness in native strength and power. They desperately need
from their communities the caring, respecting, and helping
services that will equalize opportunities so that they can
prepare themselves to function as they would like to function, and to alleviate or overcome other handicaps that
prevent them from living a satisfying life. Homemaker service, as much as any service I know, has the capacity and
the unique opportunity for doing this.

I believe that the homemaker service field must also assume new responsibilities—the kinds of responsibilities that
are a part of "coming of age." First, the field must become
action-oriented in respect to the development of related services and resources. To do this, it must share its unique and
rich knowledge of people and their needs, its long experience in organizing and providing an in-home service, and
its distinctive experience in the use of personnel selected on
the basis of personal rather than educational qualifications.
Our country and our professions are in a great dilemma as
to the most effective ways in which to reach and help fam-

ilies in poverty. The homemaker service field has a tremendous contribution to make to these families. As the nation, the states, and the local communities move more rapidly to meet widespread needs, how to organize services that meet many needs becomes an urgent question. Here, too, homemaker service has had a wealth of experience.

The stress on the use of subprofessional personnel can result in improvements in total agency services and in meaningful experiences for the subprofessional personnel—or it can end in disaster for both. We all know that overplacement is as destructive as underplacement if not more so. Some of the current claims about what nonprofessionals can do are thoroughly unrealistic, and the disclaimers of others are archaic. These different concepts and attitudes indicate the nature of the job ahead: the functions and service tasks assigned to such personnel must be useful, meaningful to the clients, and within the capacity of the personnel; requirements as to related personal qualifications must be determined; special approaches to recruitment of personnel are necessary; such staff and their functions must be integrated with other service staff and their service; and training must be carefully planned and progressively carried out. The homemaker service field has the longest and most successful experience in all of these areas and must take the initiative in making this known.

Another leadership responsibility is that of assuming active roles in assisting national, state, and local agencies in the development of services and resources that will effectively serve the needs so intimately known to homemaker service. The function of program planning generally receives the least attention from service agencies, and the trend toward diversified services provided by differentiated staff is making new demands on agency programming. For example, who knows more about in-home services than staff in homemaker service programs? Much will be lost if they do not participate in planning the in-home child care services and in determining what parents and children would best be served through in-home rather than out-of-home services.

Public Law 90-248 does offer significant opportunities to put into balance the various uses of homemaker service in meeting both social and health needs. However, there are still gaps in emphasis that will affect the achievement of fully balanced homemaker services for all who need them. I speak particularly of the lack of equivalent federal emphasis on services, such as homemaker service, for the aged, blind, and disabled. Services for them are authorized but not required, as they are for families and children. Social agencies and the homemaker service field must work to overcome the resulting inequities in meeting the needs of these groups.

It is because of my complete faith in, and feeling of closeness to, the homemaker service field that I make this final comment: the field cannot continue to be so occupied with its own service and so modest about its knowledge and capabilities. The service is now mandated to carry its leadership role beyond its own borders.

INTEGRATING THE
RURAL WELFARE DEPARTMENT
INTO THE COMMUNITY[1]

HANS S. FALCK

THE PREOCCUPATION OF THE AMERICAN
social welfare community is with the large city. The cities
call attention to increasing national effort as they harbor
the social ills that have eaten into the fiber of the very society from which they sprang. At the same time, one may
find a welfare department in almost any rural county in the
United States busy with its own caseload and beset and

[1] The data upon which this paper draws were derived from a summer project co-sponsored in 1967 by the Division of Welfare, State
Department of Health and Welfare, State of Missouri, and the School
of Social and Community Services, University of Missouri. The author's
opinions are his own and are in no way the responsibility of the
sponsors of the project.

Thanks are due to Clarence Keathley, Welfare Training Supervisor,
Division of Welfare, State of Missouri, Jefferson City, and Arthur
Nebel, Dean, School of Social and Community Service, University of
Missouri, Columbia, for their assistance in making the project possible.

plagued with the demands for help and by the inadequate resources with which to give it.

Yet, quite obviously, there are highly important differences between a rural welfare department and its big brother in the large city. A small community offers its citizens the sometimes unwanted opportunity to comprehend the totality of its dimensions. Few, if any, can be expected to visualize a metropolis with all its complexities. Many can, if they wish, encompass the small town.

A situation that exists in a small community—badly dilapidated housing that adjoins a small downtown area, for example—can be ignored only with some effort. Similarly, overt, delinquent behavior is fairly easily visible, and its occurrence subject to community awareness. Obviously, families indigenous to a given small community are known in considerable detail to large numbers of other people in an area stretching well beyond the town.

The occupational structure of small communities tends to be limited not only in its variety but also in its numerical scope. A town may have three or four physicians; it may contain half a dozen lawyers; everyone either knows or knows of the several ministers. The welfare department may be one of two or three or, sometimes, the only social agency in town. Its professional staff may have lived in the same community for many years.

A small community affords high visibility to its public officials. This is a function of high specialization of activity as well as one of rarity. When a town has only a few services of a kind, it depends on only that few. In other words, the choices that persons in small towns can make in availing themselves of community services are often few.

Nevertheless, in the small communities there are many

people in need who require all kinds of help, welfare included. Millions of persons who fall below the poverty line live in rural areas. They may be invisible to the city dweller; they can hardly be ignored without conscious effort in the small community. This is the precise problem with which the Division of Welfare of the Department of Health and Welfare of the State of Missouri has attempted to deal. The thoughts communicated here, and the program described, were formulated and developed to suggest that the rural welfare department has an opportunity to relate to the community in which it is located in ways which could be of great benefit to all involved.

Certain guiding ideas, drawn from a summary of the research that has been published, are, we believe, applicable to this discussion. In presenting them it is our purpose to suggest that some of what is known about group and organizational behavior is applicable to the use of groups in the administration of public welfare. We suggest that this would help provide a broader basis for understanding welfare departments and their possibilities.

1. The more people associate with one another under conditions of equality, the more they come to share values and norms and the more they come to like one another.[2]

2. Both the effectiveness of the group and the satisfactions of its members are increased when the members see their personal goals as being advanced by the group's goals, i.e., when the two are perceived as being in harmony. When members push their own needs, both satisfaction and effectiveness decline.[3]

[2] Bernard Berelson and Gary A. Steiner, *Human Behavior: an Inventory of Scientific Findings* (New York: Harcourt, Brace & World, Inc., 1964), p. 327. The quotations used here are summaries by the authors of social science findings in the areas of small groups and organizations and suggest succinctly the guiding ideas for this article.

[3] *Ibid.*, p. 352.

3. Strong informal groups within an organization, when hostile to its goals and methods, can effectively oppose the organization.[4]

The more supportive informal groups are, the more likely that the organization will realize its goals.

We are concerned here with the humanization of the welfare client in rural areas through integration of the welfare department with the community in which it is located. Our aim is not so much to plead for improved treatment of welfare clients; rather it is to suggest that however lofty the ultimate aim, its attainment—even if only in part—depends on a redefinition of the county directors' job perception. In addition, it depends on a rather different use of staff than is often the case at present. While undoubtedly there are departments that already do what is suggested here, and even more, some might find it useful to catalogue and reflect upon the kinds of changes that are proposed.

Attention is called to our conviction that what we call the "humanization" of the client cannot take place very effectively through good will alone. Nothing less than a redefinition of who our clients really are is necessary. This, we hold, can be achieved effectively when important modifications in the agency's major approach to people can take place. Since this would be done by all staff members, the job expectations of staff members would need modification.

Specifically, this presentation deals with the use of groups to integrate the welfare department into the community of which it is part. There are varieties of opportunities in almost every locality which could be utilized in that effort. However, the purpose is *not* "merely" to interpret present welfare procedures to a few interested citizens. The integra-

4 *Ibid.,* p. 372.

tion of the welfare department into the community is to be achieved by maximizing citizen participation in part of its operation. It would be aided in this by maximizing also the amount and kind of contact that staff other than the director would have with the community. The key to the difference between what has been the traditional interpretation of the department to the community and what we propose lies in the traditional assumption that the relief recipient is the client. We propose that the entire community—recipient, taxpayer, departmental staff, both professional and clerical—is the client. Finally, we hold that only when there is some meaningful interaction among these three can one speak of integration and, perhaps, think of a community as fulfilling its obligations to its total self by assisting its parts.

A means to at least approximate what we call for is the restructuring of the position of county welfare director into that of a community organization person. By the very nature of his job he should spend a great deal of time in the community, away from his desk. He should meet with many members of the community, individually and in groups, he should deal with varieties of people and planfully, steadily, and carefully ferret out as many points of view as possible. He should constantly search for ways to involve community persons in some proximity to the department. He must foster a sense of positive ownership on the part of the community. He ought to openly and frankly state his own views on what he thinks is good welfare performance; he should assiduously try to get people to come to grips with the realities of welfare in our society by becoming involved. Short-term public relations attempts to improve the department's image should be avoided; rather he should be prepared to make community involvement a major portion of his job, to do what is suggested and necessary. He should aim at using every opportunity to become a man with a point of view about welfare that he proposes to test out in the ongoing encounter with citizen groups.

The welfare department, as are many other governmental units, is in part a hierarchy that controls money for staff and clients. The hierarchy in public welfare is twofold: one relates to state government, of which the local welfare department could be considered a branch; the other relates to that of the federal government which has authority, and contributes financially, and expects a detailed accounting on how funds are spent. The welfare department, indeed, is often caught up in the deeply historical conflict in America between federal and state government. The welfare department is seen by some as a local expression of the local largesse of the citizenry. But some use this as an excuse for not getting involved with the federal government. It is used by some people as the rationale for the view that welfare efforts should be confined to the state or local level, where the individual citizen or small groups of citizens can quite easily control its financing and operations as well as its policy-making functions; and can resist the more distant federal government over which they have little or no control.

Most Americans probably view this double track of state and federal government as being complementary; by some Americans it is seen as highly competitive. Either way, the welfare department and its clients are often victims when the issue is honestly stated and genuinely felt; they are victimized when the issue is used as a phony excuse for inaction by an affluent society that simply wishes to keep its money for itself, assuming that welfare recipients are not part of "itself."

No matter how one defines the mission or the role of the welfare department, it is still the local arm of the federal and the state governments. It is still essentially a representative unit. There is, therefore, limited scope in the exercise of local authority. This may be enhanced, however, in so far as state departments of welfare are flexible and responsive to local conditions. One can let the possibilities that we shall describe suggest that a great many steps on the local level can be taken which can be utilized to humanize the relationship between the department and its recipients. It is even more necessary, however, for the department and the community of which it is a part to view each other as being in the service of both. The concept that governs such thinking is that the welfare worker is a servant of the public, the public at large. This public servant would do its constituency the greatest favor if it acquainted it boldly and openly with its strengths and its weaknesses. We should become accustomed to the notion that the client of the welfare department is the community, not the individual recipient. In so far as the client is the individual recipient, it is as a member of the larger community. The worker and the agency are in part the agents of the community, in part the community itself. The community is in need when any of its parts are in need. To define the clientele as individuals and families is to sidestep the responsibility of the community as a whole and the privilege that it has both to contribute to, and to be accounted to in so far as welfare is concerned.

American welfare has splintered the community. Workers are seen by the taxpayer as working for "them." By the recipients, the welfare department is viewed as representing another "them," namely, the far-distant taxpayers who provide help. The welfare department, by accepting that assignment, significantly contributes to the splintering of the community, especially the small community. We are thus at a point where there is a deep division between those who give and those who take, and the very agency that was originally established and thought by some people to be a socially integrative mechanism has become in the eyes of the receiver the agent of the hated majority in society, and in the eyes of the taxpayer little more than just as bad as the clients.

It is out of some of these and other recognitions that the Division of Welfare of the State of Missouri, with the help of federal funds, asked the writer to conduct a series of workshops in the summer of 1967 to deal with the problems discussed here.

We conducted workshops in six one-day sessions, attended by approximately fifteen county directors, their senior casework staff, and child welfare supervisors where available. The consultant traveled to six locations in the state and with the welfare department people discussed in rather highly structured one-day sessions the relationship between the welfare department and the community. We discussed frankly how the department conceives itself, how it is conceived in the community, and how it might be conceived in the future. The workshops were held during June and July of 1967 and took place in various welfare districts in the state. The format and the content were essentially similar in all six sessions. We worked out in advance the objectives that we consistently tried to realize:

1. To help welfare personnel understand the use of groups in bridging the gaps between the agency and the community

2. To help welfare supervisors and county directors see the possibilities inherent in working with community groups as well as with welfare staff toward supervisory, administrative, and educational goals

3. To demonstrate the connection between the use of task-oriented groups and the community organization responsibilities of county welfare departments

4. To discuss and demonstrate some of the specific techniques available to put what we discussed into action.

Each workshop consisted of two parts, the first being community work and the second, work with staff. The major concepts, all of which were shared with the participants, emanated partly from the workshop leader and partly from the discussion with the participants. It was most noticeable in the six workshops that the material provided and the discussions among the participants was almost completely identical from one area to another. In other words, not only are our themes valid, they appear to be universal, at least in so far as the state of Missouri is concerned. These concepts are:

1. Welfare departments, although controlled policy-wise and administratively from the State Division of Welfare, are the "property" of the community.

2. Community involvement in relation to county welfare departments is the responsibility of the community. By facilitating such involvement the welfare staff meets its responsibility.

3. Community criticism of welfare policies and practice needs to be seen as legitimate involvement calling for a positive approach by personnel rather than for defensiveness.

4. An informed community rather than an ignored or propagandized one is likely to protect the department and

its clients from unfair abuse and criticism. To achieve such a state of affairs, continuing contacts between welfare officials and community persons, including other agencies, is absolutely essential.

5. Factual and honest discussion with members of the community regarding problems relating to policy-making and administration is fundamentally important, not because it improves public relations but because the community has an obligation in relation to welfare. Problems and difficulties should be discussed openly between welfare department staff and community persons.

6. Middle-class members of the community, in addition to those of other classes, must be involved in the welfare effort.

7. Client problems need to be explained as community problems rather than only in individual terms. The problems that beset a family or a number of families must be explained in terms of what they mean to the community and not only in individual terms, thus isolating the client even further from the community that has an obligation to see after his and its own well-being.

8. The welfare staff should be portrayed as public servants who are attempting to assist communities, counties, and the states in coming to grips with those public welfare department problems that concern the community as a whole.

9. The county welfare commission and the child welfare advisory commission should be essential links between the county welfare department and the community it serves. All too often the county welfare commission is seen as a routine body, meeting more or less regularly to hear routine reports. We have evidence that the involvement of county welfare

commissions in the problems of the welfare departments is often perfunctory. Thus the staff is in a position in which it evades unpleasant answers to embarrassing questions, while the commission members shield the community from knowing the true needs of people; the truly significant discussion of welfare rarely takes place.

10. Meetings of the county welfare commission and the child welfare advisory committee should take place regularly—once a month, if at all possible, with the exception of July or August. The agenda for each meeting should be the subject of joint planning by the director and the chairman; in the case of a small commission, all members should be called for assemblage of the agenda. The chairman of the commission too often chairs the meeting only *pro forma,* and the agenda is developed by the county director with little involvement of other members, sometimes not even of the chairman.

11. Meetings should be chaired in fact as well as in name by the chairman.

12. Problems and questions arising out of meetings should be investigated with the assistance of the staff and a member of the commission or of the committee wherever feasible.

13. Commission and committee members should interpret the department of welfare to other community groups.

14. Staff should be made accessible to the lay public, particularly to commission and committee members. Efforts on the part of the director to handle all "outside" contacts are self-defeating, and especially so in small rural communities. The opportunity for staff to have intelligent contact with the community is often undermined by rigid administrative procedures that smack of defensiveness.

15. Regular meetings should be held, preferably at informal luncheons with community groups and other agency staffs, and should consist of brief presentations followed by ample opportunities for questions and answers. The identities of specific clients should be protected whenever possible, and policy and case presentations should be made without suggesting immediate solutions.

16. No staff member should be inhibited from presenting accurate information to local legislators while acting within the law so far as staff involvement is concerned.

17. There should be a reasonable amount of turnover in the membership of public advisory commissions and committees. Staff personnel should honor requests that candidates for positions be suggested, but they should also be sure that these persons would be of help to the department of welfare rather than merely uncritical or too critical because of excessive preoccupation with their own agenda.

18. Every community is an entity, including all its rich and poor, the independent and the dependent, the self-supporting and the welfare client. Communities have the right to meet their obligations; to assist them in doing so is one of the purposes of welfare departments. This means, as suggested earlier, that the community must see the problems and accomplishments of the welfare department, as far greater and far different from a mere statistical listing of clients interviewed, clients assisted, and clients discharged.

19. The job content and the perceptions of the welfare director must be subjected to rethinking in order to get him to focus on the community.

In all the discussions with the approximately ninety county directors one point was perhaps the most threatening and most controversial. Some county directors saw the suggestion that they should get into the community as an attempt to make them public relations persons. Others understood that the welfare department director's job is a legitimate expression of community change. They saw that the pseudoclerical activities of many a county welfare department director would have to undergo great change.

An immediately related problem on which we have touched briefly is the use of welfare department personnel, including clerical staff. We found in the welfare departments with which we worked that from three to thirty persons made up their staffs, including clerical employees. The use of staff, within the agency and outside, formed the content and substance of the second part of the workshops.

The content, concepts, and ideas that were discussed around this topic were:

1. All staffs are groups because of the constant formal and informal interactions of staff members.

2. All employees, including typists, stenographers, clerks, and receptionists, are members of the staff.

3. There is a high degree of functional interdependence among staff. The smaller the staff, the greater the interdependence.

4. Office personnel, who usually have the first and the last contact with clients, need training and supervision in dealing with clients as they encounter them through their work.

5. Office personnel are members of the community, and they do a great deal of talking about department work to husbands, friends, relatives, business people, and storekeepers. The more office personnel know, the better the chances that the department will be described accurately.

6. Staff meetings should include all staff members who can be made available. In large departments, section meet-

ings should be held. Office staff should be encouraged to express freely their knowledge of, and opinions on, what arises in meetings.

7. Case discussions should not be relegated to a few spare minutes at the end of staff meetings dealing with administrative matters. They should be planned for and should be handled through role-playing and presentation of techniques, and should be conducted in a problem-solving spirit.

8. Staff assignments for case presentations should be made in ample time to permit adequate preparation of material. The supervisor should act as chairman rather than as an answer-giver, and should strongly encourage intrastaff discussions rather than a one-to-one conversation between the presenter and himself.

9. Care should be taken that modifications and policy changes are shared and discussed with all staff, including clerical workers, so that the latter will feel a sense of understanding and of participation.

10. If at all possible, staff meetings and supervisory sessions should end on a note of completion, that is, with the feeling that some kind of problem has been solved, or some kind of information transmitted and understood, and that an identifiable subject has been dealt with.

These, then, are the major points that the workshops in the Division of Welfare of the State of Missouri discussed in the summer of 1967.

We shall take one particular point and develop it somewhat further. It is another example, also, of relating the welfare department to the community at large through the use of groups. Anyone who has been connected with a welfare department knows, of course, that the budgeted ex-

penses of clients do not meet their real needs. This has been
a problem as long as welfare departments have been in existence. At the same time, the impulses of a great many people in communities to provide help have been underused.
We refer specifically to the tendency of church and civic
groups to give large amounts of money, food, and toys at
Christmas time, only to forget about the welfare clients for
the rest of the year. We discussed in the workshops the possibilities of setting up year-round committees of citizens
whose business it would be to determine together with the
welfare department how it might be possible to persuade
various others in the community, particularly in groups, to
distribute these contributions of individuals and groups on
a project-defined, year-round basis. Helping with clothing,
helping with transportation of patients to clinics, visiting
sick people with Meals on Wheels programs—all are possibilities which can be pursued by departments looking for
community groups that might render services. Bringing middle-class and welfare recipients face to face has been only
partially successful because of the awkwardness, the embarrassment, and the sense of difference in dress, speech, and
values that are often experienced by welfare recipients and
by others in the communities. Nevertheless, it is possible
with sensitive planning to involve a variety of community
groups in addition to the legislatively mandated advisory
commission or committee.

Whether the staff group is involved or whether one deals
with community groups as bridging agents between welfare
departments and communities as a whole, the entire program is designed to generate a meaningful encounter between various parts of the community. In the face of often
great difficulties, it will still be necessary for taxpayer and

welfare recipient to meet in face-to-face situations despite the embarrassment and misunderstanding that could result. We believe, as recent developments in civil rights have shown, that no matter how painful or embarrassing, what we have suggested will be of little use unless we go all the way. "All the way" means that we must promote, with great courage and some trepidation, face-to-face encounters between groups of people belonging to the same community who have had almost no relevant contact with each other except through taxes grudgingly paid, public assistance reluctantly offered and shamefacedly accepted. Welfare is not, and in the future will become even less, a matter of mere financial sustenance. Obviously, the money is needed, but what is needed in addition, is a meaningful encounter in which, in a given community, the need to be on welfare will no longer be seen as the result of the recipient's immorality but rather as a state of affairs that touches the whole community. What is needed is an honest admittance by the whole community that its welfare program demonstrates its niggardliness, punitiveness, and the same restrictions that have characterized public welfare in the United States.

We know from thousands of small group studies that there is hope in the face-to-face encounter among people, and it has become even clearer to me that it is the only hope. Sooner or later we must face up to the fact that some of us need help and some of us do not, and that there ought to be no shame, no sense of accomplishment, in either receiving or in giving. This, of course, and the broad involvement of community groups, is the seed for making welfare much less painful for millions of Americans than it has been over the generations. That seed is one that can bring to realization the fact that regardless of race or color, men and women have a right to reasonable and well-paid employment. To be on welfare is a financial state of affairs, but it can also be a means by which those who require assistance can gain some self-respect in being accepted for the human beings that they are, as accepted as those in the community who through luck or achievement or fate have not found themselves in need of public help.

The essential characteristic of small group life is social confrontation. The quality of that confrontation determines its usefulness. There is nothing inevitable about the way in which it turns out in a given group. With a worker who knows how to maximize its benefits, great rewards can ensue. Even in a mass society, and perhaps because it is a mass society, the advantages of face-to-face interaction must be cultivated and guarded. That is what the project we described is all about. Although riots have been concentrated in some cities and have not taken place in small towns, what American can possibly blind himself to the need to do something about the dreadful distance between himself and so many others?

WHY PUBLIC WELFARE
NEEDS VOLUNTEERS

CYNTHIA R. NATHAN

THE OFFICE OF CITIZEN PARTICIPATION HAS been created in the Social and Rehabilitation Service of the Department of Health, Education, and Welfare, but citizen participation is not new. It is as old as the New England town meeting, as old as the Senate of Rome, as old as the dawn of civilization when man first worked cooperatively, sharing his labor and the fruits of his labor, deciding in common how he would be governed.

Citizen participation is our heritage and our birthright, a foundation of our way of life. It finds expression in the jury of peers. It is manifest in our boards of education, in our boards of health. It is revealed at every level of our government. The elected mayors and aldermen of cities, the elected governors and legislators of states, the elected President and Congressmen of our nation, are evidence enough of our democratic base.

But democracy rests on the premise of participation and on the promise that channels for that participation will be accessible to all. Reactions of remoteness are common among all segments of the citizenry. The middle class has felt itself shut off from intimate involvement in the agencies which serve the poor. The poor are among the minority groups which charge that they have been shunned and excluded, deprived and denied. Long inactive, the poor have awakened to their vested right to speak out, to petition their government. They are joining the professional lobbyist. They are groping their way through a maze of officialdom. They are appearing before aldermen, state legislators, and Congressional committees to make their needs known.

Many outside the power structure have felt alienated, estranged, and impotent. Members of some groups, finding strength in each other, have organized. Once organized, they have demonstrated, sometimes with violence. Protests center on the right to self-determination and the wish for self-fulfillment. Students, feeling cut off from academe, have seized control of universities and imprisoned administrators. Encapsulated ghettos have erupted in arson and looting. Recipients have staged sit-ins at welfare departments, on one occasion imprisoning the welfare staff, destroying the office, and continuing their riot on adjoining streets.

There is divisiveness and a growing dissatisfaction with the institutions that society has created to solve its problems. The displeasure permeates the political and social arena. And it strikes at the agencies of government.

Public welfare is no exception. Criticism and attack come from all sides. The recipient fears and resents the agency which was created to serve him. He charges that it does not meet his needs. He points out that it disregards his opinions. He sees the larger society as callous to his human strivings. He sees the agency as failing to involve him in decision-making, even in those areas in which the agency has discretion and in matters which affect the very core of his existence. He is embittered.

And what of the affluent? They have a similar disaffection for the public welfare system. The affluent believe that they created the institution of public welfare to discharge their responsibilities to the poor. They do not approve of the manner in which these responsibilities are being discharged. They too feel shunned and excluded from the policy-making process. They believe, on the one hand, that their tax funds are misspent, that "chiseling" and fraud are rampant, that the able-bodied should be denied aid, that children should not be brought into this world by parents who must turn to the affluent for support. Yet, on the other hand, they will not turn their backs on a malnourished child, nor deny the necessities of life to the unemployed, nor fail to nurse the sick, to house the old, to care for the disabled. The affluent see America as the land of opportunity, and most of them are eager to lend a hand to those who reach for it. But they are frustrated. Their outstretched hands have not been seen. They do not know how to lift the veil which conceals them. They do not know how to cross over to the world of the poor. The Office of Citizen Participation can provide the channels.

On rare occasions the affluent have come to know a family in poverty. Then, they have been critical of public welfare, not for what it gives, but for what it denies. Then, the fear of fraud is superseded by the shock of finding out how little is provided. Our mailbags burst with letters decrying the existence of hunger in a land of plenty.

The problems of public welfare may never be solved through the system as we know it today. But solutions may come through a wide involvement of the citizenry.

I believe that the people of this great land welcome participation in problem-solving with the poor. And I believe that the affluent are willing to contribute their time and skills, their vision and resourcefulness in the service of the poor.

It has been said that men will part least willingly with their wives and their money, and sometimes with their money last. Yet billions are given annually in voluntary contributions. Suburbia funded the poor who encamped in Resurrection City near the banks of the Potomac during the Poor People's March in 1968. Government workers took their annual leave to care for the children of the marchers. Physicians found time to examine the poor. Teachers volunteered to hold classes. Teen-agers made sandwiches. Churches housed those who had no other shelter. Bathtubs in private homes worked overtime. It was a magnificent example of the commitment, the conscience, the generosity of a nation. The poor, the middle class, and the rich joined hands in helpful giving—make no mistake, the local poor gave, too.

Divisiveness can give way to unity of purpose, hostility to cooperation. There is indeed more that unites than divides us.

The oneness grew more apparent daily in the Poor People's March. And amazing though it may seem, there was no attempt to seize control by the citizens who gave so much. The poor people elected their own officials, chose their own marshals. The middle class did not even try to usurp their power or to destroy their pride.

Do you know what the poor chanted as they shuffled the two miles to the halls of Congress, to buoy their spirits and give them courage to face the awesome legislators? "I am somebody. I am somebody. I am somebody."

Self-government, autonomy, self-direction characterized the organization of Resurrection City. This self-determination is what the poor seek in their relationships with public welfare. This self-determination is what they have achieved in the Poor People's March. This self-determination is what they have achieved in their welfare rights groups which are now active in 60 cities in 30 states, with 6,000 dues-paying, button-wearing members. And the welfare rights movement is just beginning to take hold. A volunteer body itself, the National Welfare Rights Organization has welcomed the voluntary help of welfare workers and of faculty members from schools of social work. It has welcomed voluntary aid from settlement houses and councils of social agencies. But it maintains its independence in policy-making.

Let me try to make the reactions to imposed benefits come alive, as they did for me. And then let us see if we will not conclude that public welfare needs citizen participation to help recipients achieve the self-realization of which they are capable. Let us see if we will not conclude that the efforts of volunteers will have the greatest impact if they are in answer to the felt needs, the formulated and expressed needs, of the applicants for, and recipients of, public assistance. He serves best who honors the opinions of the person he would serve. He serves best who listens before he speaks. He serves best who grants what is needed. Only when the poor have been given a voice in the management of the agency which seeks to help them, which exists to help them, will the real objectives of public welfare be fulfilled. Only in this way can self-respect be advanced. Only in this way can initiative be promoted. Only in this way can the image of self-confidence be furthered, and ultimately independence be achieved.

Public welfare has not always known how to provide this partnership with the poor, for it flies in the face of tradition. Traditional goals are a comforting help, but traditional methods may be a disastrous hindrance. We have come a long way from the Christmas basket, but we must never forget the Christian spirit. We have come a long way from doing *to* the poor. We are doing *for* the poor. We must now do *with* the poor. So, if it is only a question of changing a little preposition, one could argue that we are not too far from success.

Doing *for* the poor is so much a part of our orientation and our basic methods that the welfare agency is not alone in its failure to seek the counsel of the recipients of services. Even that champion of self-actuation, the Office of Economic Opportunity, can fall into the trap of decision-making on behalf of its clientele rather than with its clientele. Sargent Shriver tells the story of a bright young antipoverty worker, eager to provide for the comfort of both mothers and babies, who suggested the installation of cribs in the waiting room of a model community health clinic. Once installed, the cribs were rarely used, and when they were, the chorus of howling babies pierced the air. The mothers knew what was wrong. "You can't," they said, "put a baby in a crib he senses is strange and leave him alone. Why didn't you get rocking chairs?" Now I may be wrong, but I think rocking chairs also cost less than cribs.

While I was visiting a county welfare office in a North Central state, I happened on the angry demonstration of a welfare rights group. Now, the county director of this agency is sympathetic, understanding, and resourceful; more than that, he is sensitive. His devotion to the cause of the persons he serves is unquestioned. Yet his recipients were irate, infuriated. The reasons for their anger were many, but they had a common core. Their concept of which needs should take precedence was different from the concept of the county on the one hand and that of the agency on the other. The county had allocated funds for the improvement of its public buildings, and the welfare agency had succeeded in getting its fair share. Its unattractive quarters were to be remodeled and air conditioning was to be installed. The agency saw this as a victory: staff and clients had won the symbolic respect of the community.

But the recipients fumed. "What," they shouted, "do we read in the newspapers? Air conditioning? Air conditioning when we do not have refrigerators? There are 300 families who have no refrigerators. Our babies' milk will spoil while you sit in air-conditioned comfort."

The county director, of course, was powerless to have the county rechannel funds from a building appropriation to an appropriation for household furnishings. The recipients were not aware that their demonstration should have been directed to the county body which allocated funds, and timed to coincide with its budget hearings. And the wider community, the community which pays the bulk of the taxes and approves the distribution of public funds, I am certain, was unaware of the need for refrigerators.

Let me cite another example from this same county. The county director had won funds for a satellite office in an area where many recipients lived. His objective was obviously the convenience of the poor. "What," raged the recipients, "do we read in the papers? A contract has been let for this new suboffice. What we need in that spot is a day care center. We are leaving our children in rickety buildings, with makeshift care. Nobody gives us what we want." Were we again providing cribs instead of rocking chairs?

I was present at a confrontation at HEW by a delegation

from one of the more affluent New England states. The
story was the same. "We do not want foster day care," said
the mothers, "unless there is better supervision. Let us help
to supervise, if you cannot do the job. Let us have a voice in
choosing the homes our children will go to. We can pick
our doctors. We worry when we know that someone takes
our children merely for the money. Give us day care centers.
And do not make a rule that says, like the one we have now,
that because there are so few day care placements available,
only the mother who takes an agency-referred job or training can have her children go to a day care center. You are
taking away our independence. You are forcing us to wait
for the agency to find us jobs. If we find our own we suffer
for it." And so it goes.

The need for participation in decision-making is apparent. The need for an informed citizenry is urgent. HEW,
through the Office of Citizen Participation, has moved to
make both a reality. Congress has been our stanch ally. The
Social Security amendments of 1967 make it mandatory for
every state which wishes to claim federal financial participation in its public assistance and child welfare programs to
include in its state plan provisions for the use and training
of volunteers, and each state must use volunteers to assist
advisory boards. To insure that volunteers will come from
all segments of society, provision is also made for the payment of some. This is really a part payment for services, not
to be regarded as a reflection of the worth of the services
but rather as a token. The payment is designed to make it
possible for even the poorest of the poor to serve in partnership with more affluent citizens. Where services to recipients
are given, the same expenditure-matching formula will
apply. The federal government encourages a broad program

of volunteer services by underwriting 75 percent of its cost.

The mandatory requirements for a program of volunteer services are contained in provisions popularly referred to as the Harris amendments, named for Senator Fred Harris, of Oklahoma, who introduced and justified them. Let me excerpt from Senator Harris. His full remarks may be found in the *Congressional Record* of October 16, 1967.

I believe our welfare programs can and must have more of the human touch. . . . I find that there is great and growing hostility on the part of the poor against the effect and operation of many of these programs. . . . Overworked social workers come to be regarded by many welfare recipients as persons who only enforce the law against the poor, rather than the friendly, helpful advisors they should be. . . . I have found . . . the lingering feeling in the minds of many . . . that the poor should be punished for their poverty. . . . This volunteer program would start to fill a desperate need which exists in this country for middle-class people, personally, to know more about the poor people, their living conditions, their problems, their needs, and their desires. . . . As American citizens become more aware of these real facts . . . their innate decency compels them to become involved and to support solutions to the problems of poverty. . . . The social service volunteer program is designed to provide another and very important avenue for all American citizens, young and old, to give of themselves to others . . . and they will respond to widened opportunities for service . . . as VISTA, the Peace Corps and other such programs so clearly show.

Commenting on the Harris amendments, Mary Switzer, Administrator of the Social and Rehabilitation Service, stated: "We should, and now we must, seek and utilize citizen involvement in our programs. It is my hope that the new Office of Citizen Participation, which we have established, can be of help to state and local welfare offices in utilizing the tremendous resource of citizen energy, skill, and interest, including the involvement of the poor themselves."

The Office of Citizen Participation prepared materials which should prove helpful to the states. There is a job description for a director of volunteer services at the state and local level who would work with an advisory council of recipients to determine the help they seek from volunteers. The director would be a catalytic agent who brings recipients together and then helps them to establish priorities of the services they wish to receive. Their considered opinions and their requests would be transmitted to a committee of volunteer representatives who would undertake to meet those requests which seemed feasible. The committee of volunteers would always be free to suggest services that they regarded as important, but no services would be given until they had been approved by the recipient council.

The director of volunteers would also chair a staff committee of agency personnel sensitive to the needs of recipients. This committee would suggest pertinent volunteer services, and these too would be presented to the recipient council. Where individual recipients had requested individual services, every worker would be expected to report directly to the director of volunteer services, who would submit these requests to the volunteers.

The Office of Citizen Participation intends to maintain a flexible approach. We are serving as a clearinghouse of information and calling attention to county and district programs which are innovative, imaginative, and successful.

We hope to outline a basic training program for volunteers and to publicize the urgent need for volunteers, while at the same time we assure social workers that no attempt will be made to interfere with or to supplant their casework plans. Rather, we see the volunteer effort as supplementary and complementary to agency obligations. We see it as furthering the goals of the agency, the staff, the recipients, and the entire community.

We see this program as a channel which will open the way to participation, which will fulfill the promise that participation will be open to the poor and the nonpoor. The nonpoor, through their intimate involvement in the life and problems of the poor, and in the functioning of the public welfare agency, will develop acute awareness. They will understand the hopes and the dreams of the young poor. They will understand the frustrations, the shattered dreams, the nightmare life of the parents of poverty's children. They will understand the limitations of the agency. They will understand how to help.

We see this same channel leading the poor to participate in community affairs, leading them to determine their own destinies, so that their feelings of alienation may be replaced by the knowledge that the community is not callous. The volunteer will always symbolize the community's concern.

May I predict that the informed volunteer will become the advocate of the poor? May I predict that the informed citizen will question society's values and actions and attitudes in giving our tax dollars to the affluent owner of fertile corn land, so that this land may be idle, while denying these same dollars to the tenant farmer who is forcibly idled because he can no longer till this same land?

The informed volunteer who sees the apathy of hungry children will question why hogs are slaughtered and discarded. The informed volunteer will join hands with the impoverished parents of America's children and will echo their pleas in the halls of Congress so that the dreams of youth may be fulfilled. And in so doing, we shall have made one more move toward erasing the divisiveness which has until now separated the affluent from the poor, citizen from citizen.

NEXT STEPS FOR CHILDREN[1]

WILBUR J. COHEN

THIRTY YEARS AGO Franklin D. Roosevelt
remarked that the destiny of American youth was the destiny
of America. In the years since then, considerable progress
has been made in shaping that destiny. The majority of
American young people have enjoyed the benefits of a growing, prosperous nation; they have had an increasing share
of material comforts; they have more educational opportunities; and their chances of healthy childhood have increased.

Progress has accelerated within the current decade, and
Congress has produced a series of legislative enactments that
have done more for our young people than previous measures in any other period in our history: the Elementary
and Secondary Education Act; the Higher Education Act;
the Economic Opportunity Act; the Child Health Act; and
the Child Nutrition Act.

[1] Revised from the original and reprinted by special permission of
the Child Welfare League of America from *Child Welfare*, XLVII
(1968), 440–45, 491.

An unprecedented investment has been made in American children and youth during the 1960s. In the fiscal year 1968, this aspect of federal expenditure alone totaled $12.8 billion—more than triple the amount spent in 1960. And those dollars have been well spent, as the following statistics illustrate:

Head Start and other preschool programs have provided learning opportunities and health care to more than 2 million disadvantaged children in the last three years.

Nine million children in more than 19,000 school districts are getting special help under the Elementary and Secondary Education Act of 1965.

The high school dropout rate was reduced by more than 25 percent in five years.

Federal grants, loans, and work-study programs are helping nearly 1.25 million young Americans through college—*five times* the number aided in 1963.

About 466,000 young people, ages 18–22, who are in school, received $479 million in social security benefits during the 1968–69 school year—an amount greater than the scholarships at all the colleges and universities in the United States.

More than 2,000 college graduates have joined the Teacher Corps to teach deprived children in our urban ghettos and our depressed rural areas.

The infant mortality rate fell from 25.2 deaths per thousand in 1963 to 22.1 per thousand in 1967, a decline of 12 percent in four years.

Within four years, the number of children suffering from diphtheria, polio, tetanus, and whooping cough was reduced by 50 percent.

The incidence of measles among children aged 16 and
   under fell by 90 percent between 1964 and 1967.

In spite of our affluence—a society accused of pampering
some of its young with overindulgence and permissiveness
—the fact is that we have failed millions of children and
youth who are still the captives of poverty, disease, squalor,
and ignorance.

Over 12 million children in the United States under the age
   of 18 live in families too poor to feed and house them
   adequately.
Over 10 percent of our young men between the ages of 16
   and 19 are out of school and out of work.
Over 10 percent of American children are referred to a juve-
   nile court for delinquency before their eighteenth birth-
   day.
Nearly one million young people drop out of school each
   year.
Nearly 750,000 babies—almost one in every five—are born
   each year to mothers who receive little or no obstetric
   care.
Teen-age pregnancies are on the increase.
Almost one half of the children in the United States under
   the age of 15 have never been to a dentist.
Suicide ranks as one of the leading causes of death among
   children.
The problem of drugs and narcotics reaches beyond the
   ghettos into the middle-class suburbs.
Nearly 10 percent of all school children have serious emo-
   tional problems.
Large numbers of American youth drop out of meaningful

activities, while others clamor for more active involvement.

The communications gap between the generations, races, the rich and the poor, the cities and the suburbs widens.[2]

We can and we must cure these ills if we are to preserve our heritage and protect the future of this country. This is our responsibility to a generation that we must prepare for adulthood in a world of complexities which will far outweigh those of ours today.

I do not have solutions for all of these problems but I do have some ideas about where we can and must start. We must start with the very young and with the poorest of our children, because it is with them that both the hope of fulfillment and the tragedy of failure are the greatest. In health, in education, in all of human experience, the early years are the critical years. Ill-health, inability to learn, and emotional problems, often contracted in childhood, cripple for life and damage the next generation.

Research. As Secretary of Health, Education, and Welfare, I have established a high priority on programs that will promote healthy childhood development.

We begin with research. The National Institute of Child Health and Human Development is focusing on the broad areas of child health, mental retardation, the effects of nutrition on human development, and a number of other related inquiries, in order to advance our knowledge of how to prevent disease and promote healthy growth.

As we seek new knowledge on the maturation of the

2 Present needs of children and youth are described more fully in *Federal Programs Assisting Children and Youth* (Washington, D.C.: Social and Rehabilitation Service, Children's Bureau, U.S. Department of Health, Education and Welfare, 1967).

human personality, we are at the same time moving to apply this knowledge more quickly and directly to the lives of people.

Family planning. An area that has had our special attention, and one in which we have made some remarkable breakthroughs in the past three years, is that of family planning. Six years ago, we could only whisper about the subject. In 1967 the federal government helped to bring family planning information and services to about 500,000 women. Yet even this effort reached only a fraction of the 5 million women who want such assistance but who cannot get it because they lack either money, education, or access to a physician.

We hope to reach one million of these women. President Johnson recommended to Congress that HEW's appropriation of $25 million be more than doubled—to $61 million —so that by 1969, 3 million women would have access to family planning services.[3] By the end of this decade we hope that such services will be available for every woman who desires them.

The expansion of family planning services and the prevention of illegitimacy rank among our highest priorities. A study made in 1967 showed that for 8.2 million women in the low-income bracket there were 451,000 unwanted pregnancies.[4] We must do everything possible to make every child a wanted child. This is the greatest blessing any child can receive.

Another study showed that out-of-wedlock pregnancies

[3] "Health in America," Presidential Message to the Congress, March 4, 1968.
[4] Arthur A. Campbell, "The Role of Family Planning and the Reduction of Poverty, *Journal of Marriage and the Family*, XXX (1968), 237.

among very young girls are increasing, as the number of persons in this age range increases in our population.[5] One community reported, for example, that during 1966, 40 percent of the patients in its maternity and infant care program were nineteen years old, or younger; 68 percent of these were not married, and 25 percent had had a second or third illegitimate pregnancy by the age of seventeen.[6] It is estimated that if current national trends continue, approximately 70,000 girls under eighteen years of age will have a child born out of wedlock in 1970.

Programs focused on young unmarried mothers must be widely extended if we are to interrupt the cycle of educational failure, absence of normal family life, and continued illegitimacy. These girls require a comprehensive program of health, education, and social services.

There are now in existence thirty-six new projects that relate to pregnant school-age girls.[7] Most of them followed from the experience of the Children's Bureau demonstration project in the District of Columbia, which provided comprehensive services to approximately 500 such girls. Many more efforts of this kind are needed to prevent this teen-age tragedy.

Maternal and child health. We are also moving ahead to improve maternal and child health programs. Under the Child Health Act of 1967, we are developing new ways to

[5] "Changing Trends in Illegitimacy," *Monthly Vital Statistics Reports Highlights from the National Center for Health Statistics,* XV, No. 3 (1966), 1. See also Elizabeth M. Goodman, "Habilitation of the Unwed Teen-age Mother: an Interdisciplinary and Community Responsibility, *Child Welfare,* XLVII (1968), 274.

[6] Unpublished data of the Children's Bureau.

[7] Marion Howard, "Multiservice Programs for Pregnant School Girls," U.S. Department of Health, Education, and Welfare. Social and Rehabilitation Service, Children's Bureau, 1968.

reach mothers and children in slum areas. Proposed amendments would further strengthen our efforts to provide every
needy mother and infant with comprehensive health care
by the 1970s.

We must take steps now to assure that far more adequate
health services are provided for children of all ages. Many
children in the ghettos have handicaps that can be easily
remedied with early detection and care. If we could reach
these children at an early age, we could begin to break the
ugly cycle of poverty and attendant ill-health, poor education, unemployment, crime, and illegitimacy. We have
asked Congress for additional funds to provide screening,
prevention, and treatment for more children in low-income
areas. We are taking these services into the areas where the
people are rather than waiting for the people to seek out,
and perhaps never find, the care they need.

We need a bold new effort in the entire field of child
health. Proposed amendments would give us a good start. I
believe, however, that we are also going to require some
kind of a "Kiddie Care" program, in addition to Medicare
at some time in the future.

Early education. We are also giving high priority to innovative early education programs for children. We recently
established a federal interagency panel on early childhood
programs, to guide the development of preschool and day
care programs. This is a first step toward the improvement
and expansion of all early childhood programs financed by
federal funds. Coordinator and chairman of the panel is
Jule M. Sugarman, Associate Chief of the Children's Bureau. As former director of Head Start, Mr. Sugarman has
had extensive experience with health, social services, and educational programs for disadvantaged, preschool children.

There is a need for substantial and continuing federal support for the care and training of children during those critical preschool years when their problems should be found and treated and their potential nurtured. We want to develop the whole child, and to work with the parents in order to raise the quality of life of the poverty-stricken. We want to assure that federal funds will guarantee for these children the kinds of experiences that will enable them to develop the confidence, motivation, and skills they will need.

The panel has given attention to: the development of the joint day care standards required under the 1967 amendments to the Economic Opportunity Act amendments of 1967; coordinated funding in cooperation with state and local agencies; and broadened and improved training and technical assistance efforts.

The 1967 amendments to the Social Security Act require adequate day care for the children of mothers who receive welfare and who are referred for jobs or training. Regulations have been issued to the states to safeguard children and insure that high standards are maintained.

Day care centers should provide creative, stimulating, and motivating experiences for both the child and parent, and we propose to do everything possible to reach that goal.

Other educational programs. Our ultimate contribution to our children's future will be through education to prepare them with knowledge and skills to compete in a highly technological world. We must continue to strengthen education at all levels.

HEW established a Central Cities Project to bring the best programs in compensatory education to target areas in certain cities. We have asked Congress for funds to expand the Teacher Corps so that 4,000 dedicated young men and women can go into the central cities to help children who need extra attention.

In today's world, twelve years of education are no longer enough. We would like to see at least fifteen years of publicly supported education—from preschool through junior college. We would like to see vocational and technical education strengthened. We need more experimental projects at all levels. And we must remove the current imbalances in the quality of education among the 20,000 school districts in the nation.

We have issued new guidelines, under Title VI of the Civil Rights Act, for eliminating segregation in schools. These will have special impact on schools in the Northern cities.

The Office of Education has been encouraging better community-school relations and has been stepping up its work in this area. We would like to see the schools develop into community centers, open twelve months a year, eighteen hours a day.

To meet these needs a vast expansion of both public and private support is required.

Social security and welfare. A family income sufficient to provide a decent standard of living is, of course, basic to the needs of every child. The most desirable assurance of family income, in most cases, is a well-paying job; but many families must rely on social security and public assistance as their major source of income.

In recent years, social security has been substantially strengthened. The 1967 amendments provided the largest increase in the amount of social security benefits given since the enactment of the Social Security law in 1935.

About 3.5 million children, many of whom were living in poverty, benefited directly from the increase, but too many are still impoverished.

In a nation as prosperous as the United States, where the gross national product has been increasing at an average annual rate of 5 percent, there is no reason why social security beneficiaries, children included, should not share in the expanding prosperity. We can, and we must, steadily improve the program to keep pace with the nation's growth.

The public program most directly focused on the needy is public assistance. Although the AFDC rolls have been steadily increasing, only a fraction of the nation's needy children receive benefits under this program, and the benefits are wholly inadequate.

HEW has made a number of proposals for improvements in the welfare program:

1. We recommended to Congress repeal of the controversial AFDC freeze on federal payments contained in the 1967 amendments.

2. We expect the Supreme Court to rule on lower court actions that invalidate state residency requirements, and the restrictive man-in-the-house rule. In the meantime, we have urged the states to eliminate the man-in-the-house rule.[8]

3. We have urged the states and localities to improve the availability and accessibility of their services, and to use neighborhood people constructively in their programs. We

[8] *Editor's note:* On June 17, the Supreme Court in King *vs.* Smith, invalidated "man-in-the house" or "substitute parent" rules. On June 21, the Department of Health, Education, and Welfare issued a directive to the states that this ruling means that "eligibility of children for AFDC because of deprivation of parental support can only be determined in relation to a child's natural or adoptive parent, or a stepparent who is legally obligated to support the child."

In April, 1969, the residency requirements were outlawed by the Supreme Court.

search for ways to improve the communication gap between the poor and the rest of the community.

4. We have urged localities to initiate emergency welfare assistance programs that we hope will make it possible for needy people in emergency situations to get help promptly, without the stigma generally attached to welfare. This program, authorized by Congress in the 1967 amendments, provides that the federal government will pay one half of the cost of any cash emergency payments to an individual or family for thirty days, and three quarters of the cost of any services to them. The payments may be in the form of grants, loans, or goods and may be made without extended investigations.

5. We have also recommended a number of other ways that the welfare system may be made more humane and more adequate.

The President's Commission on Income Maintenance is studying a number of ways to overhaul the existing welfare system. It is too early to say what the recommendations of this Commission will be. While we await these recommendations, I believe we must make some radical changes in the scope of coverage, in the adequacy of payments, in the way present welfare payments are administered, and in building incentives to independence. One way to accomplish this would be to establish a federal system of income payments with eligibility, the amount of payments, and appeals determined on a nationwide basis. We would then overcome many of the problems of inequity, variations between states, and fiscal inadequacy, all of which have plagued the welfare system that we have today.

Whatever system we finally adopt, we must take some steps promptly to do away with poverty and the handicaps it imposes on our people. Programs for the 3.5 million children born each year must be a part of any long-range so-lution. The future of these children is where our hopes lie. We want them to have every chance to grow and to reach their full potential.

Manpower. One of the most serious problems facing us in the years ahead in the entire social welfare field is the acute shortage of manpower. This problem can best be met through an increased use of nonprofessionals. Although we must train more professional people, we must at the same time provide meaningful new careers for thousands who want to participate in programs that affect their lives. We must tap the large reservoir of potential manpower among neighborhood residents, youth, minority groups, retired peo-ple, and others who cannot now participate because of res-trictive standards and certification procedures.

White House Conference. The decade of the 1970s is rap-idly approaching, and with it will come a host of new prob-lems accompanied by new opportunities. By 1970, over half of the population of the United States will be under twen-ty-five years of age. New and increased demands will be put on health, education, and welfare services. Automation, technology, and scientific advancement will call for greater efforts in building bridges between the world of learning and the world of work. Changing social values will require improved communication and understanding between the generations. Youth will demand an even greater role in the decisions affecting their lives, and institutions will have to be made more flexible to accommodate those demands.

These are some of the problems that will confront the White House Conference on Children and Youth when it convenes in 1970.

As Staff Director of the White House Conference, Dr. Jo-seph H. Douglas will lead the planning efforts for what we believe will be one of the most important conferences since the first one was called by President Theodore Roosevelt in 1909. We are confident that the conference will direct its attention to new goals based on the vast changes taking place nationally.

I offer for consideration at that conference a reaffirmation of rights for children of today and tomorrow:

1. The right of every child to spiritual and moral training, to help him meet the pressures of life
2. The right of every child to understanding and respect for his own personality
3. The right to a safe, wholesome home of love and security, free from conditions that thwart his development
4. The right to be wanted and well-born
5. The right to a healthy childhood
6. The right to community recognition of his needs, protection against physical dangers, moral hazards, and disease
7. The right to an education that, through the discovery and development of his individual abilities, prepares him for life; and through training and vocational guidance prepares him for a living that will yield him the maximum of satisfaction
8. The right to teaching and training, to prepare him for parenthood, homemaking, and the rights of citizenship
9. The right to grow up in a family with an adequate standard of living and the security of a stable income.[9]

I pledge myself to the fulfillment of these rights for every child—those already among us, and those yet unborn. It is our most challenging task for the next decade!

[9] Based on "The Children's Charter," developed at the 1930 White House Conference on Child Health and Protection.